DOG MOM

How to Be the Best Mama to Your Fur Baby

Christine Amorose Merrill

Illustrated by Krishna Chavda

Ulysses Press

Published by:
Ulysses Press
P.O. Box 3440
Berkeley, CA 94703
www.ulyssespress.com

ISBN: 978-1-61243-792-7
Library of Congress Control Number: 2018930787

Printed in Korea by Artin Printing Company through Four Colour Print Group

10 9 8 7 6 5 4 3 2 1

Acquisitions editor: Casie Vogel
Managing editor: Claire Chun
Editor: Barbara Schultz
Proofreader: Renee Rutledge
Front cover design: Krishna Chavda
Interior design and layout: Malea Clark-Nicholson
Background patterns: © Nadezhda Molkentin/shutterstock.com, © L. Kramer/
    shutterstock.com
Author photo: © Jillian Wishart

Distributed by Publishers Group West

TO MOM,
FOR TEACHING ME THAT DOGS ARE ALWAYS
PART OF THE FAMILY.

. . . .

CONTENTS

· · · · · · ·

Hello!..7

PART I   FIRST THINGS FIRST
What Makes a Dog Mom?...11

PART II   BECOMING THE NUMBER ONE DOG MOM
The Different Types of Pup Parenting.................................19

PART III   AFTER ADOPTION
Creating a Strong Dog-Mom Bond.................................39

PART IV   STAYING HEALTHY AND LOOKING FAB
Fun, Fashion, and Food...59

PART V   BEING BEST FRIENDS
How to Go Everywhere Together.................................87

PART VI   BUILDING YOUR COMMUNITY
It Takes a Village to Raise a Pup.................................113

Conclusion...126

Acknowledgments...128

About the Contributors...128

HELLO!

· · ·

My name is Christine, and I'm a certified "crazy" dog mom. I come from a long line of devoted dog moms: Women in my family have always had dogs, and have always treated their fur "kids" just as well (if not better) than they've treated the children and husbands in their lives. I grew up in a household where the dog was considered a member of the family. Although I was an only child, we always had a dog—and that dog was basically a sister to me.

My dad jokes that when he dies, he wants to come back as me or the dog; we've both been equally spoiled by my mother. My husband recently said the same thing in regard to our dog, which means I must be doing something right in raising our pup.

My husband and I brought home a tiny pug puppy in the spring of 2016. Gertrude Rose Merrill—affectionately known as Gertie or simply Gert—is a smush-faceed, curly-tailed, wriggly, and wrinkly ball of personality. I quickly and effortlessly turned into a full-blown crazy dog mom, complete with a nanny cam to watch her every move while I was at work, an @cestgertie Instagram account, and a trunk stuffed full of dog outfits and costumes (especially impractical when you consider the minuscule size of our Brooklyn apartment).

My camera roll shifted from cityscapes and far-flung beaches (we lived in New York City, but I moonlighted as a travel writer) to 100 percent pug: photos and videos of her sleeping on my husband's shoulder, cuddling with her stuffed turtle, proudly parading down the sidewalk with a leaf in her mouth, and riding on the subway for the first time with puggy eyes wide.

We joke that we moved from New York City to San Diego to give our pug a better life, but in reality, it's not that far from the truth. As much as I struggled with subway delays, harsh winters, and our insanely expensive rent, I also worried about how our long working hours, sidewalks covered in slush and salt, and lack of proximity to a park affected our pup.

My husband often reminds me I'm being ridiculous. And in my heart of hearts, I know that my pup has a better life than most. But a dog mom always wants what's best for her pooch!

Although I grew up always having a dog sister in the house, being a mom to my "dog-hter" changed me in ways I didn't expect. I have become the woman who whips out her cell phone to show off photos of her pup to friends and strangers, whether or not they've expressed even a hint of interest in dogs, and mine in particular: "Here she is after a bath! And here she is in her pirate costume, isn't she adorable?" I've obsessed over sleep schedules and poop consistency and the attentiveness of her midday walker. I've left parties early to come home and snuggle on the couch with her. I spend vacations checking in on her via nanny cam and swooning over how cute she is via the stockpile of photos and videos on my phone.

More than anything, I love her more intensely than I ever thought possible: being a dog mom will do that to you.

LOVE

IS A

FOUR

LEGGED

WORD

PART I

FIRST THINGS FIRST

What Makes a Dog Mom?

WHAT IS A DOG MOM?

· · · · · · · · · · · · · · · · · · · ·

First things first: A dog mom is not the same thing as being a dog owner. Anyone can have a dog, and anyone can keep a dog fed, healthy, walked, groomed, and even reasonably happy.

But being a "dog mom" is something special. It goes above and beyond just keeping your pup alive—although in those first few moments of bringing a tiny, wriggly puppy home, just the responsibility of that can feel overwhelming.

Being a dog mom doesn't mean you don't have human babies, or don't want "real" kids of your own. It also doesn't necessarily preclude you from being a cat lady. And it's not strictly a millennial thing. I learned many of my dog mom ways from my mom and my grandma.

Being a dog mom mostly means that you treat your pup like a full-fledged member of the family, not just a pet. Members of the family are invited along on vacations, not stuck in kennels. Their birthdays are properly celebrated with treats, toys, and a party. They watch Netflix snuggled up next to you on the couch, not relegated to the cold, hard floor. You have ongoing conversations and inside jokes with them, and a long list of lovable nicknames for them. And most importantly, the pup children of dog moms are loved so incredibly fiercely; you'd do just about anything to keep your pooch by your side.

CHECKLIST:

ARE YOU A DOG MOM?

Do you...

- Treat your dog better than you do most people?
- Dress your dog up in costumes—and not just on Halloween?
- Run an Instagram, Facebook, Snapchat, or YouTube account on your dog's behalf?
- Have a nanny camera set up to record your pup's every move?
- Have a camera roll that is 99 percent photos of your fur baby?
- Ensure that your pup's schedule is regularly packed with their favorite activities, like afternoon sessions at the agility training club or laid-back mornings at their favorite dog park?
- Have approximately a million "pet" names for your pooch?
- Take your dog to as many social events with you as social etiquette will allow (or maybe just beyond that limit)?
- Cancel plans with friends because you'd rather hang out with your pup?
- Set aside special time for you and your pup to bond one-on-one?
- Have regular, ongoing, and intimate conversations with your doggo—in private and in public?
- Supply a regular rotation of new toys designed to keep your pup feeling mentally stimulated, physically active, and emotionally snuggled?
- Worry about your pup's happiness and entertainment when you're not at home, and perhaps leave the TV or radio on to make him or her feel less alone?

If you've answered yes to most or all of the above...congrats! You're a dog mom! Welcome to the ridiculously fun club of crazy rearers of spoiled fur babies.

LIVING THE DOG MOM LIFE

I'm not going to lie: The dog mom life is pretty darn great. Being a dog mom means that you always have the *best* best friend around, even when you're fighting with your husband or wife, your friends are too busy with their own lives to hang out, or your boss is driving you crazy. Your pup sidekick is always available and ready to make you smile or to lick the tears off your face, and hanging out with you is always number one in their book of favorite things.

The truth is that, when you become a dog mom, everything changes. Your priorities shift from what's best for you to what's best for your pup, and your mind space is overcome with the daily work of keeping your fur baby happy, healthy, and tired—especially if you brought home a helpless little puppy! You will discuss pee, poop, and going out schedules far more than you ever thought possible, and you'll happily fork out oodles of cash for the best food, toys, and vet care your paycheck can buy.

Coming home to your dog is the best part of your day, and the most mundane of errands are more fun with your four-legged friend along for the walk or ride. Even when your fur babe is driving you a little crazy with a little (or a lot) of mischief, you still can't help but want to forgive them immediately and snuggle them. Those puppy-dog eyes really can make up for a lot!

MY KIDS

HAVE

PAWS

DOG HAIR, DON'T CARE

As awesome as being a dog mom is, there are definitely some drawbacks.

Odds are that your house, car, and every item of clothing you own will instantly and constantly be covered in dog hair (unless you lucked out and fell in love with a hypoallergenic pooch).

You'll get used to rolling out of bed and onto the streets of your neighborhood before you have time to put on makeup or real clothes. Yup, you woke up like this and you're not ashamed; you're the naturally beautiful and makeup-free mother of the most beautiful pup around. A dog mom's gotta do what a dog mom's gotta do!

When you're sipping piña coladas and soaking up the sunshine on a beautiful beach somewhere, you'll be texting your dog sitter to ask for yet another photo of your fur baby. From now on, the best part of vacation will be boarding the plane home to be reunited with your pup.

On the street, strangers and friends won't stop to say hello to you or ask you about your day, but they'll instantly bend down to pet your pooch. They'll want to know what his name is, how old he is, and what kind of dog he is. If you have a puppy, be warned: there's no use wearing headphones any more.

Your credit card statement will be filled with charges to pet stores, grooming boutiques, and dog walkers—no one said being a dog mom came cheap! Although some of those charges will be deemed necessities—a responsible dog owner can't skimp on food, poop bags, and recommended vaccines!—you'll also know that some of those splurges (ahem, BarkBox) are worth it to keep your pooch delighted.

PRO DOG MOM TIP

Although this book is focused on all the incredible dog moms out there, it doesn't mean that there aren't a ton of other important family members involved in the lives of each and every pup. Here are a few important dog family members we'll mention.

Dog Moms: That's you! Fiercely loyal ladies who will do anything for their fur babies.

Dog Dads: Although I disagree that dogs are just "a man's best friend," the relationships between dudes and dogs are pretty tight. Your dog may have a dog dad (or more than one) in her life.

Dog Aunts and Uncles: Maybe this was the first step in your dog mom journey, being your BFF's go-to dog sitter or being the one who's always up for a walk with your sibling's pooch. Building this community is crucial, not only for your dog's well-being but also for yours.

Dog Grandparents: This might be where your love of dogs began. Your parents (aka your pup's grandparents) are likely to spoil your dog just as much as you do, if not more.

Dog Siblings: If you have more than one dog offspring, you'll soon learn that the sibling bond between dogs who live together is unmistakable, even if they aren't the same breed, gender, or size! And, of course, if you have human kids: they can be a huge part of their dog siblings' lives.

PART II

BECOMING THE NUMBER ONE DOG MOM

The Different Types of Pup Parenting

BEING THE MOM
YOUR DOG DESERVES

. . . .

Here's the good news: Your dog is going to love you—
always, forever, unconditionally. So, so, so much.

It's not hard to be a mom that your dog will love. Make
sure they have a full bowl of food and water every night, a
nice walk through all of their favorite smells each morning,
and a comfy place to snooze every night, and they'll think
you're the best dog mom around.

But being the mom your dog deserves? That's a whole
other story. That's a tale of treats and toys, playdates and
patience, unlimited love and unparalleled energy.

And in some ways, it's an impossible task. The sort of
unconditional love and loyalty that your dog displays can
never be matched by our impatient and imperfect human
foibles. You (understandably) will be frustrated when your
puppy has an accident on your favorite rug, or tries to get
your attention by chewing an expensive and irreplaceable
vintage purse.

However, don't be too hard on yourself. The work
you put into being an A+ dog mom often spills over into
other areas of your life: striving to be a better dog mom
can make you more patient with coworkers, more loving
toward your partner, more playful with your friends, and
even more appreciative of your own mother!

FINDING YOUR
FOUR-LEGGED OTHER HALF

The first step to becoming a dog mom is finding your perfect pooch sidekick(s)!

It might be a super-intentional choice, or a pup might just fall into your lap. It's hard to predict how it will happen for you. Some of my most intensely organized and plan-ahead–type friends brought home their dog children on a whim after walking by a rescue event on the sidewalk, and more laid-back, haphazard friends spent many months on outreach and applications in search of their dream dog.

I spent years agonizing over when my life would feel "ready" enough to bring home a dog. I lived in a series of tiny apartments crowded with roommates in New York City, and spent a ton of time in airports and hotels across the globe for my side gig as a travel writer. When my husband and I first moved in together after a few years of pug-obsessed dating, we still waited about six months before we introduced the third member of our family. I don't know if we were 100 percent ready for the trials and tribulations of being dog parents: I still traveled a lot for work, we both had long commutes from our fifth-floor apartment in Brooklyn to our demanding jobs in Manhattan, and neither of us had ever owned a puppy.

However, one of my favorite life philosophies is to leap when you're *almost* ready. You're rarely going to feel 100 percent prepared to do anything that's big enough to matter: get married, have kids, bring home your first dog, even jump out of a plane. That's why on your first skydive, the instructor might count down: "5, 4, 3, 2..." and push you out of the plane at 2!

Bringing home a dog is life-changing, and any dog mom knows it's not a decision to be taken lightly. But there's no perfect time to become a dog mom and there's no perfect way to raise your pup. Whether you've expertly planned out the exact day you'll welcome your fur baby home or the stars align to make it a bit more spontaneous, the only thing for certain is that the real fun starts once you've got a pooch by your side.

My husband now comments that he's surprised that I didn't already have a dog when I met him; I'm so obsessed with our Gert! Although I would have loved to have had a dog sooner, I'm just grateful that I got to become a dog mom when I did.

If you've decided it's time to become a dog mom, do your homework! Make sure you understand where your pup comes from; ask a lot of questions and be ready to give your pup all of your love. There's no going back once you bring that fur baby home!

RESCUE MOMS

There are so many incredible dogs of all shapes, sizes, personalities, and special needs in shelters, foster homes, and rescue groups out there just waiting to find their fur-ever homes.

Rescue moms are in a win-win-win situation: They reap all of the fur babe benefits like unconditional love and undying loyalty, save a deserving pup from a more dismal fate, and support the important and relentless work of animal rescue organizations. Y'all deserve a medal, but instead you just get the four-legged love of your life!

Rescuing can also be a smart financial choice. Many rescue pups are already properly vaccinated and spayed or neutered before you adopt, so you will save a hefty chunk in vet fees. Also, the fee for a rescue dog usually goes straight back into the shelter's operating costs to save even more deserving pups.

Of course, it's impossible to know a dog's full history when you rescue—especially if you rescue an adult dog. One of the most stressful parts of adopting a dog is not knowing what its start to life was like: Does it have triggers, health issues, or behavioral problems that you don't know about? If you're adopting a puppy, just how big is it going to get? Take a good long look at those paws if you're living in a small space—the bigger a puppy's paws are, the bigger that dog will be when he or she grows up!

Just as it's important to ask a lot of questions about the dog and its provenance when you're deciding to adopt, it's equally crucial to answer all of the adoption application questions honestly. Both sides want to make sure that the pup is going to end up in his or her paw-fect home for life. Shelter workers don't want to send the most energetic pup home to someone who works long hours and can't guarantee lots of playtime; that's a recipe for a failed dog-mom relationship.

When I was growing up, both of my family dogs were adopted from the local shelter: Susie, a pit bull–Australian shepherd–chow chow mix was 16 weeks old when we brought her home; and Annie, a Staffordshire terrier–Australian cattle dog mix, was just under a year. Both were delightful additions to our family—full of love and energy, and never short on snuggles—and their unique looks only added to their charm. Susie had a purple tongue, a curled tail, and a brindled coat. Annie is white with black spots; she has one blue eye and one brown eye, and one of her ears stands straight up while the other flops down.

Because of our incredibly positive experiences (and the many, many experiences of my friends and proud rescue dog moms everywhere), I'm a big believer in, and a financial supporter of, the mission of the American Society for the Prevention of Cruelty to Animals. I am also a strong proponent of neutering and spaying your pets. Although there are ASPCA and Humane Society shelters across the country, there are also breed-specific rescue groups or independent nonprofit animal shelters in most major American cities and small towns.

Whether or not you're a rescue mom yourself, if you're looking for a worthy charitable cause to support, consider making a regular donation of funds or supplies to your local animal shelter or a favorite dog-rescue group. A monthly gift that is just the price of a couple of lattes (or one new toy for your spoiled pup) can go a long way in an animal shelter. The financial help will help to make sure all pups who deserve a loving fur-ever home are able to find one, and extra supplies like dog food, treats, and toys will free up funds to be used strategically!

YOU CAN'T
BUY LOVE,
BUT YOU CAN
RESCUE IT.

PUREBREED MOMS

Some people are more drawn to certain breeds than others, whether it's because of the type of dog that the mom grew up with or a particular breed being better suited to their current lifestyle.. Just like people, some dogs are more suited for camping on the lake for a weekend versus camping out on the couch all day.

Case in point: I'm a pug person! Despite neither of us owning a pug before, my husband and I bonded early about our shared crazy love of those smush-faced, curly-tailed, charming, and mischievous pups, and we both knew that our tiny Brooklyn apartment and long working hours wouldn't be the best fit for a bigger or more rambunctious dog. We decided to buy our pug puppy from an independent breeder in Staten Island. Patti "Pug Lady" Pugz is well-known in the pug community in New York City as being a true lover of pugs. She legally changed her name to Patti Pugz (she showed me her driver's license as proof!), and her house was covered in more pug paraphernalia than I knew existed in the world. She's also a registered breeder with the American Kennel Club. When we visited, we knew that this self-proclaimed "crazy pug lady" would give us a good pug. Although we extensively debated whether or not to rescue, we're so happy we decided to bring home a baby from Patti Pugz. And now we're dedicated members of the Pug Rescue of San Diego group, which has regular pug (and pug people!) meet-ups around town.

If you do opt to get a purebreed pup, be aware of the physical and mental health burdens that can be placed on little babes that are born in puppy mills and sold in pet stores. It's highly recommended to visit a breeder before you agree to purchase one of their puppies. You'll want to make sure that the mama and papa dogs are healthy and happy, and that the environment is clean and conducive to raising good pups. Your site visit is also a gut check: Does this feel like a good place for my pup to start life? If not—if you have even an inkling of doubt—please, please, please (I beg of you!) don't spend your money there.

Things to look out for if you are dedicated to getting a purebreed pup:

Make sure the breeder is American Kennel Club–certified. Not only will you be able to establish lineage if you're interested in showing your dog, but you'll also know that the breeder takes its breeding and health guidelines seriously. Double-check that the breeder is actually listed on the American Kennel Club website, and see if the individual is a member of any local breed-specific clubs.

Ask for references. Getting in touch with the families of previously placed pups can give you insight into the ongoing health and behavior of the dogs, and you'll be able to confirm there aren't any lingering issues to be aware of. Bonus: You might be able to have some family reunion playdates! We're in touch with three other pups from Gert's litter (who coincidentally all live on the same block in TriBeCa), and the pups are always stoked to see each other (and we pug people can bond over Patti Pugz's pug obsession).

Ensure that the puppies are getting all of their necessary shots on time. When you pick up your puppy, check that they're up to date on all necessary vaccines. Ask for proof of vaccinations and vet appointments to take with you to your vet. You'll want to go to your own vet within 48 hours of picking up your puppy, and you should make sure that all of the puppy's paperwork is up to date.

INDEPENDENT/SINGLE DOG MOMS

All my single dog moms, put your hands up! Being a dog mom can be one of the most rewarding relationships possible: Dogs are excellent listeners, genuinely love to snuggle, can make you laugh even when you're mid-sob, and will forever fiercely protect you. They're great companions on the couch or out on the town, and will do anything to make you happy! Who wouldn't want a partner like that?

Although there are challenges to being a single dog mom, there's nothing that can't be solved with a committed community of dog aunts. Having a neighbor, nearby friend, or a reliable walker who can step in when you're held up late at work or when you're traveling is key, and finding other dog moms to swap dog-sitting duties with can be a huge relief as well. The benefits far outweigh the difficulties: you'll forever have a cuddle pal who doubles as an excellent judge of character for whenever you meet a potential fur baby daddy.

When my mom was working as an FBI agent in Baltimore in the late 1970s (real life, and probably enough stories for a whole other book!), another agent brought in a box of puppies that had been found on the side of the street. My mom wasn't necessarily planning on a pup of her own—she was an independent lady with a demanding job—but she decided she couldn't turn away a furry companion in need. Amanda was my mom's first pooch and best sidekick. They drove across the country to move to California together in my mom's tiny Volkswagen Rabbit. Being a single dog mom wasn't necessarily in my mom's life strategy, but the right pup can sometimes overrule the best-laid plans. Bonus: Amanda was the most dedicated and incredibly protective dog sister anyone could have when I arrived several years later!

The best part of being a single dog mom: You will always and forever become first in your pup's heart. No competing with a partner for the dog's love; you will give them 100 percent of their meals and take them on all of their walks and basically be their number one bud for all time, no matter who else comes into the picture later.

COPARENT DOG MOMS

As someone who intentionally waited to get a dog until she was living with her boyfriend, I can only really speak to the partnered-up-with-a-dog lifestyle choice. Spoiler alert: It's not always going to be sunshine and rainbows, and there will likely be some heated words exchanged. It's all part of the pup parenting game!

Deciding to raise a pup together is a huge step in any relationship. You're not only committing to each other for the (hopefully very long!) lifespan of your pooch, but you're also promising your fur baby that they'll be raised by two equally invested and super-loving dog parents. As daunting as that can seem, it's also so much fun to be able to share the experience with someone else. As the Swedish proverb goes, "Shared joy is a double joy, shared sorrow is half sorrow." You'll always have someone to laugh with over your pup's hilarious antics, and someone to commiserate with when your fur baby acts up. My husband and I still regularly pull up a little video I made of Gert's first week at home, and laughingly reminisce at just how little she was. And our current favorite topic of conversation is when will she get a little pug sister?!

If you decide to make the leap, check out my coparent survival guide later on (page 49). And the best part of the whole co-dog-parenting thing: you always have a guaranteed dog walker when you just need a night out with your girls!

AGE AIN'T NOTHING BUT A NUMBER

. . . .

There are pros and cons to bringing home a doggo at any stage of life, but there's a paw-fect age for every type of dog mom.

Puppies. These fluffy babies are undeniably the most adorable *and* the most work. I personally believe that the level of cuteness is directly related to how much mischief they cause. No matter how rascally they get, you can't be angry at those (literal) puppy-dog eyes. Puppies will demand a lot of attention (sometimes good, sometimes bad), and a dog mom knows that she's going to have to sacrifice a lot of time, energy, and money at the beginning of a young pup's life.

The upside is, those little whirls of fluff are like unformed balls of clay that you can carefully and con-sistently train into your dream dog. Although it's tough at the beginning, the reward is a pooch that you can watch grow up into a paw-fectly well-behaved pup.

If you do opt for a puppy, get serious about discipline and training from the get-go; you're laying the foundation for the rest of your dog's life!

Young and middle-aged dogs. More mature than a puppy, but not quite in their prime, dogs at this stage of life can be the best of both worlds. You do run a bit of a risk if you don't know much about their history, but if you can find a dog who's already house-trained and already schooled in the basic commands, you can save yourself a lot of DIY-discipline-induced despair.

Senior dogs. Older dogs are often the hardest to place in fur-ever homes, but this can be an incredibly rewarding experience. They're so full of love, and they're perfect snuggle buddies. If you're more excited about curling up on the couch all weekend than stacking your day with outdoor activities, or if you work long hours, an older dog might be a better choice than a rambunctious pup.

PRO DOG MOM TIP

Of course, the world is conspiring to make life easier for dog moms everywhere. Apps like Wag and Rover allow you to book dog walking or dog sitting on demand. Both can be accessed on the go via your smartphone, and both offer reasonably priced services. You no longer need to ask friends or neighbors for favors at the last minute!

Wag provides free lockboxes to secure somewhere near your front door, and it truly is on-demand: most walks occur within 30 minutes of booking on the app, although you can also schedule them ahead on a regular or one-off basis.

Rover relies more heavily on crowd-sourced reviews and is home to plenty of enthusiastic dog lovers. Many people on Rover aren't professional walkers or dog sitters; they just love dogs, and are happy to walk them or open up their home to a four-legged friend for the weekend.

If you're worried about the medical issues and associated financial burdens that often come with a senior pooch, consider adopting from an organization like Susie's Senior Dogs. It's a nonprofit that works to bring attention to the plight of homeless senior dogs, and will often utilize donations to help with special training sessions or vet care. Many other rescue groups are also set up to help with canine medical bills if you are willing to adopt an older or special-needs dog. Don't be afraid to ask!

HOME IS WHERE THE DOG IS

Here's the good news: a dog is going to feel at home wherever he or she is with you, and a good dog mom can make even the tiniest apartment feel like a pup-friendly palace.

I don't think anyone is going to deny that having a backyard makes it easier to have a dog. If you can shuffle over and open a door in your pajamas first thing in the morning, that can instantly take one thing off your to-do list. The backyard always has plenty of interesting smells to sniff out, circles to run in, and potential critters to catch. On the flip side, you rarely see people lovingly and regularly walking their pooches around the neighborhood like the city folk are forced to do!

Raising your fur baby in a tiny apartment in a big city can be a blessing in disguise. It encourages dog moms to be extra active and creative in how they ensure their pups get enough exercise, and in turn, that can be a great way for you to work more steps. Bonus: dogs in big cities are often much friendlier, or at least more at ease, with a wide variety of pooches because they're exposed to so many in tight quarters.

There are also some breeds that are better suited to apartment living. One of the main reasons that we were so excited about having a pug in New York City is that they are masters of apartment living: They prefer a nap-heavy lifestyle (i.e., they sleep up to 80 percent of the day), and their squat size makes them and their accoutrements fairly unobtrusive in a small apartment. There's a reason you see so many pugs, French bulldogs, cavalier King Charles spaniels, shih tzus, and Malteses in big cities; they're all especially well-suited for life in small apartments.

Larger dogs need bigger crates or beds. They go through more food more quickly and often can knock things over just with a tail wag. However, it's worth doing some research. You may be surprised to learn that enormous Great Danes and large but gentle Greyhounds are usually super calm and their exercise needs are moderate, so they can also make excellent apartment dogs. You just have to have a big enough apartment for them to fit in!

But if there's one really good reason to buy a house, it's not to settle down in the suburbs and have kids, or because you need a break from city chaos. It's so the dog children have a backyard to frolic in! Just don't stop walking them or taking them to the park because they finally have a space of their own: pups can get lonely, bored, and depressed without an opportunity to smell all of the new smells around the neighborhood or to make new dog friends.

CHOOSING A NAME

· · · · · · · · · · · · · · · ·

Just like the name of a human child, the name you give your pup will have lasting consequences. You will want to make sure it's something that you truly love and that paw-fectly suits your fur baby! Odds are, you're going to be saying it all the doggone time.

My mom has two rules for a dog name: it should be two syllables, and you can't feel ridiculous yelling it in public. I'd also add that it should be a name that brings you some degree of joy, and that has the possibility of nicknames.

Also, it's true that dogs can feel embarrassment, shyness, and humiliation. Think twice before giving your dog a name that will get a lot of laughs, unless you want your pup to have a complex!

If you're considering having human children of your own one day, my mom also strongly cautions against using your favorite name on the dog. Case in point: She named her first dog Amanda. She wanted to name me Amanda, too, but my father refused to name his firstborn child after the dog.

NAME INSPO:

CELEB DOG MOMS & THEIR FAMOUS POOCHES

BAYLOR: Selena Gomez's rescued husky mix

TUCKER: Charlize Theron's (fourth!) rescued mixed breed

KAROO: Hilary Swank's rescued Jack Russell/Corgi mix (found while on the set of a movie in South Africa)

DOT AND ZELDA: Zooey Deschanel's rescued pups (who are actually sisters!)

OLIVIA, GEORGIE, AND FRANCIS: Jane Lynch's Lhasa Apso, Wheaten terrier, and Australian shepherd mix

REN: Emma Stone's golden retriever

ESMERELDA AND KENOBI: Anne Hathaway's chocolate lab and rescued terrier mix

SHIRLEY, NORMAN, AND RUBY: Kaley Cuoco's pit bulls

FINN: Amanda Seyfried's Australian shepherd

POPPY, RUBY, AND BEBE: Sandra Bullock's pups, all with special needs

DOLLY AND SOPHIE: Jennifer Aniston's pit bull and white German shepherd

OLIVER: Rihanna's Maltese poodle mix that she found and brought home during a night of clubbing

CHIP: Serena Williams's Yorkie

PEPPER, PIPPA, AND PUDDY: Chrissy Teigen's bulldogs

MUGSY: Zoe Saldana's rescued white terrier mix

LUKE, LAYLA, SADIE, SUNNY, AND LAUREN: Oprah's two golden retrievers, cocker spaniel, and two springer spaniels

PART III

AFTER ADOPTION

Creating a Strong Dog-Mom Bond

FALLING IN LOVE AT FIRST BARK

· · · · · · · · · · ·

The moment when you meet your fur baby is an unforgettable one, whether it's a still squirmy just-born pup or a full-grown sweetheart ready to be adopted into his or her fur-ever home with you. Tears may be shed, a million photos may be taken. Okay, let's be honest: Tears definitely will be shed, and a million photos absolutely will be taken. There's no shame in your dog mom game!

Falling in love with your pup is instantaneous. Once you know, you know! And once you find your chosen fur baby, life will be forever changed—in the best possible way.

ESTABLISHING QUALITY MAMA AND PUPPY TIME

A lot about dog owning can feel like a chore (because it kind of is): needing to walk the dog, feed the dog, tire out the dog so that he or she will sleep well at night. It can be easy to become overwhelmed and exhausted by the daily minutiae of keeping your pup happy and healthy.

To keep yourself happy and healthy, it can be helpful to shift your attitude toward those sorts of daily tasks. This is your special time to bond with your pup!

Beyond that, it can be rewarding to set aside "bonus time" for the two of you to bond. This can be as simple as cuddles on the couch (perhaps accompanied by wine and Netflix!), a dedicated weekly trip to the park or beach, a "yappy hour" together at an al fresco bar, or perhaps something like a special mommy-and-me *doga* class (aka yoga for dogs).

For me, Gert's first walk in the morning is sacred mommy-and-me time. I wake up early enough so that we can spend a solid 30 minutes together before work. After my alarm goes off, I take a quick shower and then wake Gertie up in her crate. She's usually still sleepy and a little grumpy—I often have to drag her out of her warm, snuggly spot to put her leash on, though she gets some pep in her step as soon as we head outside into the crisp morning air. We try to mix up our route most days—it's a nice way to explore our new-ish neighborhood, too!—but we usually end up at a little park where I can let her off-leash for a quick romp around on the grass. Once she's done a few rounds of zoomies (in other words, set herself up verrrrry nicely for a long morning nap) and possibly made a few new four-legged friends, we head home. Sometimes I use that time to listen to my favorite daily news podcast, but other times I leave my phone at home. It can be a refreshing reset to the day to focus on the fresh air and my fur baby.

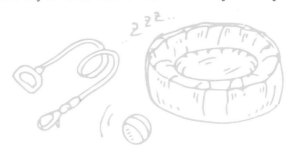

SCHEDULE INSPO:

A WEEK IN THE LIFE OF THE DEDICATED DOG MOM

SUNDAY	Eliminate the Sunday scaries with a serious pampering session: Light the fancy candles, draw a bubble bath, put on a sheet mask, paint your toenails. And, of course, dedicate some spa time to your pup! Give him or her a luxurious bath and blow-dry, trim nails and brush teeth. Make sure that your pup is looking and feeling their finest.
MONDAY	Set the alarm a little early, and start the week with a rejuvenating long walk through the neighborhood before you tackle your to-do list. Consider leaving your phone at home; a mini digital detox allows you to bond more deeply with your pup and enjoy your surroundings, as well as begin the week on a relaxed and de-stressed note.
TUESDAY	Treat yourself to a baking session: perhaps a batch of peanut-butter cookies for yourself, and a set of a homemade pumpkin-spice treats for your pup (see page 84 for the recipe). Your fur baby will be stoked to lick out the batter bowl!
WEDNESDAY	Give yourself a hump-day break with an evening of Netflix and chill. Order some takeout, splurge on a bully stick for your fur baby, and settle in for a marathon snuggle session on the couch.
THURSDAY	Head to your favorite neighborhood dog park after work to run out some of that pent-up midweek energy, and perhaps find a few new pup friends and fellow dog moms to make weekend plans with!
FRIDAY	Celebrate the start of the weekend with a yappy hour for you and your pup. Enjoy a cocktail al fresco, and order something off the doggy menu for your fur baby: perhaps apple slices drizzled with peanut butter? Invite a few other dog moms and their pups to make it a paw-ty!
SATURDAY	Om your way into the weekend with a morning doga class. It's a paw-fect way for you to get in a good stretch and some extra one-on-one bonding with your own downward dog. Namaste!

THE BEST PART OF EVERY DAY: COMING HOME

Perhaps the number one reason to get a dog is that there's no better feeling than coming home to a pup who is so incredibly happy to see you! It simply can't be matched. Every day when you come home from work, your fur baby is going to act like you've just returned from a years-long mission to Mars in which they have missed you every single moment of the day. I swear, the best and most intense tail-wagging, bum-shaking shimmy is reserved for when you walk through the door after a long day. Don't cheat yourself out of this end-of-the-day reward, even if you still have things on your to-do list or you need to get dinner on the table; give yourself a moment to snuggle and appreciate this delightful reunion with your fur baby.

THE JOY ONLY DOGS CAN GIVE YOU

Puppies truly are nature's antidepressant. It's impossible to be upset when a little fur baby is licking your tears away.

It's hard to describe just how comforting and joyful a pup can be, in good times and bad. Those little bum wiggles as they rush toward you, the snuggling up in the crook of your arm—your dog will quickly figure out the best way to make you smile, and will make it his or her mission in life to make you as happy as often as possible.

I remember having a rough day at work once and collapsing on the couch in a burst of tears once I got home. Gertie immediately intuited that I was upset, and quickly jumped on my chest and started smothering me in kisses. It was enough to stop my tears and make me laugh. All this little creature wants is to make me happy! If I'm not at home to take advantage of a snuggle session, sometimes just remembering one is enough to turn my frown upside down. And if that fails, a scroll through my pug-filled camera roll or her latest Instagram posts will usually do the trick.

NAMASTE HOME WITH MY DOG

THE EMOTIONAL TOLL

. . . .

For all of the joy that a fur baby can bring, raising a sweet, well-behaved, responsible citizen of a pup is not an easy task. It takes discipline and dedication, early mornings and sleepless nights, and it can cause a heck of a lot of non-joy-induced tears.

Tiny puppies have tiny bladders, and to be quite honest, tiny brains, and tiny teeth that can inflict giant damage. They're still figuring out this whole living-with-people thing, and although they want to please you with their whole enormous hearts, a lot of mistakes will be made. These mistakes can result in chewed-up (expensive) couches, peed-on (antique) rugs, destroyed (irreplaceable) paperbacks.

Even if you adopt an older dog, there can be some serious adjustment time as your pup navigates a new environment, discovers all sorts of delicious things to chew, and gets used to the whole, unconditional love and care that you're offering.

The bad news? The first few months are the hardest, and they are *tough*. Every dog mom with a wonderfully behaved, incredibly sweet pup has plenty of nightmare stories to tell when it comes to training and acclimation.

A lot of dog moms—myself included—can be a little impatient when it comes to wanting our fur babies to be immediately perfect. We want them always to behave as well as our staged Instagram posts make them look!

The good news? It gets easier! And all of the hard work that you put in at the beginning pays dividends in the form of a very good doggo.

MISADVENTURES IN DOG PARENTING

Fun little story of how it played out for us: Right as we were gearing up to bring home our puppy, I got an incredible opportunity to travel to France for work. The only caveat? I'd be leaving just three days after we came home with a 12-week-old pug puppy. My then-boyfriend was incredibly supportive and encouraged me to say yes. I scheduled a red-eye to Cannes, but there was still about an hour or so between the time I left for the airport and the time when David would get home from work.

We followed advice from some dog-training book that instructed us to create a space connected to her crate where she could do her business. I placed her crate in the doorway of the bathroom, and then put a few newspapers down on the bathroom floor. When I left, I plopped Gert down in the bathroom, left David a nice bottle of whiskey on the dining room table as thanks, and hoped for the best. As I was boarding a couple of hours later, I got a call from David. When he arrived home to our apartment, he discovered a scene worthy of a dog-raising horror movie. Gertie had—so sweetly—managed to poop on the newspapers I laid down for her in the bathroom, but had then promptly walked right through it... and then tried to valiantly escape from the bathroom by hopping up on her hind legs and scratching the walls, door, toilet, and bathtub with her poop-covered front paws. So, when David returned home, not only did he have an enthusiastically unruly pup to deal with on his own, but he also had a whole bathroom to scrub and sanitize. The bottle of whiskey was deemed a necessity, not a luxury.

Now we laugh about the "horror movie scene" of poop that awaited him in the bathroom, but at the time, it felt like this insurmountable challenge. Were we going to be wiping poop off our walls and cleaning a poop-covered pup for the rest of our lives? Even though we told ourselves that we weren't, it sure felt like a daunting possibility at the time.

THE COPARENTING SURVIVAL GUIDE

. . . .

Raising a fur baby with another person can be an incredibly rewarding shared experience. It can be a world of support and inside jokes, and a pup can be a source of joint entertainment that provides far more laughs than any Netflix romantic comedy.

However, as a dog mom, you are not about to let anyone mistreat your baby (or even fail to spoil them properly), even if that person is your spouse, life partner, roommate, or best friend. Hell hath no fury like a dog mom annoyed.

Eyes will roll. Tears will be shed. Fights are inevitable. Patience will be tested. Coparenting a pup is a quick and dirty way to learn *a lot* about each other.

From one dog mom to another, here are my top coparenting survival tips (via hard lessons learned):

Dog parenting is fun! First and foremost, remember that this whole having-a-dog-together thing is pretty darn fun. Make time to play together as a family, and don't forget to laugh when your pup does something hilarious. Send those entertaining moments via text, or create a shared online photo album, if one partner isn't at home for the fun.

Identify your strengths and weaknesses. Figure out where each other's strengths lie, and play to those. One partner might naturally be more patient and consistent when it comes to training; let that person take the lead on nightly sessions to teach commands like "stay" and "roll over." You, on the other hand, might be the natural keeper of your family's Amazon cart and weekly schedule; in that case, consider yourself in charge of keeping the dog food stocked and dog walker booked.

Compromise, compromise, compromise. From agreeing on names and Instagram handles to deciding whether or not the dog should sleep in your bed, there are going to be a lot of pup-rearing choices to be made, and you and your partner might stand firmly on opposing sides at times. Be willing to negotiate and compromise, especially if it's not a deal-breaking issue for you (and it is for your coparent!).

Poop: everyone better get used to it. You're going to be talking about it a lot! And don't forget to invest in an end-of-the-world-worthy supply of stain removers, poop bags, and laundry quarters.

There's a learning curve for speaking dog. Early puppy parenting is 99 percent trying to accurately interpret the signs of needing to go out. You'll both be wrong at times. Even if it ruins your rug, don't let it ruin your night. Buy a set of "potty bells" to (eventually) take out the ambiguity of your pup standing (anxiously? calmly?) by the door, and put that end-of-the-world supply of stain remover to good use.

Offer to take the night shift. Decide on "shifts" that make sense. Because I'm naturally up before the sun and my husband is more of a night owl, I'm in charge of the first morning walk and breakfast, and my husband is responsible for dinner and going out before bed. And if one partner travels a lot for work (she said, raising her hand guiltily), pitch in every once in a while to do a whole day of walks and feedings when you both are home. Your partner will appreciate the break!

Your baby isn't perfect. So don't blame each other for mistakes that the dog makes. This is so tempting, and impossible to avoid completely. Remember what I said about tiny bladders and tiny brains: It's not (usually) their fault. But it doesn't help to get mad at each other for the mistakes that the dog is making.

PRO MOM TIP

For the dog partners, dog dads, and dog dates out there, here are a few survival phrases that will make your life just a little easier.

- "I would love to go on a W.A.L.K. with you and Duke in the pouring rain."
- "Yes, you definitely should buy 15 different Halloween costumes for Lula."
- "Move over. Gertie needs to sit in this tiny nook between us on the couch. It's her favorite spot!"
- "Can you hold FaceTime in front of Buddy so I can say hi? Wait, make him come back!"

Don't keep score. Nothing in life, and certainly nothing in relationships is going to be perfectly 50-50. There will be weeks when you're able to step up and take the pup to the dog park a few extra times, and other weeks when you'll lean heavily on your partner to pick up the slack. It will all even out in the end.

Be consistent. If you've jointly decided not to give your fur baby any table food or allow sleeping in your bed (even if you really want to—compromise, remember?), don't sneak snacks or snuggles when your partner isn't around. Not only does it create a weird atmosphere of disrespect to your partner, but it also confuses your fur baby!

You're in this together. Remember that you're both learning how to co-pup-parent together. Even if one or both partners have had dogs before (or neither of you has!), this is the first time you're doing this together. Be extra communicative, appreciative, and upbeat.

WHEN PEOPLE JUST DON'T UNDERSTAND

Being a dog mom isn't easy, but it's a labor of love. However, not everyone sees it that way. People, especially those without dogs, may have a hard time with your obsession. I've found there are a few types of people and some smart ways to deal with their negative vibes.

FRIENDS WITH KIDS

A dog mom can totally be a current or future mom of humans, too. Pups love having actual children siblings! And being a dedicated and enthusiastic dog mom doesn't necessarily mean that you never want to have "real" biological, adopted, or stepkids of your own someday. Being a great dog mom is often an excellent indicator of nurturing, caring, and general good parenting skills.

Sometimes a dog is the first step on your journey to a family with offspring of your own, and other times, having a single fur baby or a pack of pups is all the mothering you need. No judgment here: every dog mom knows herself and her desires and decisions best.

But if you're a happy mom to a fur baby with no other little ones on the way, you will find that moms of human babes are sometimes dismissive of dog moms. It can tough, especially if you're in the midst of a challenging spurt of housetraining or if you've intentionally chosen a life as a dog mom and not a human mom. Your pup parenting matters, too!

Although it can be tough to bite your tongue (What? Just me?) when a mother of a human child belittles your status as a dog mom, I like to focus on all of the things that are truly wonderful about just having a fur baby (at least for right now!). You don't have to worry about saving for college (and obedience school tuition is a steal, comparatively), and it's socially acceptable to leave your pup at home alone whenever you want a night out on the town. Dogs don't go through a teenage phase where they ignore you or get embarrassed by your antics, and they're always grateful when you give them dinner (no matter what's on their plate!). Your dog will never refuse to take a nap (more likely, they'll be begging for more naps!) or throw a temper tantrum. Even if they can't take care of you in old age, you know your pup will be the most loyal and most loving companion for as long as you both live.

Here's one of my favorite mantras for just about every experience that proves that comparison truly is the thief of joy: I'm not saying it's right, I'm not saying it's wrong, I'm just saying it is. Remember that your mama friend is just as obsessed (okay, maybe a little more) with her babe as you are with your fur baby. This whole parenting game isn't a competitive sport. Coo over her baby, but don't be offended if she doesn't swoon over yours. It is what it is, and there's no use losing sleep over it.

DOG MOM

FRIENDS WHO AREN'T "DOG PEOPLE"

As exciting as bringing home your fur baby is, it can throw a major wrench into your lifestyle, particularly when it comes to social events. And this shift in priorities—especially at the beginning, as you're figuring out a new normal in your schedule—can definitely affect your friendships. Perhaps the most challenging can be dealing with friends who—gasp—aren't even dog people. Whether they're cat ladies or just not animal lovers, it can be tough to communicate that, um, no, this isn't just a dog. This is my child and she should be treated with love, care, and respect!

The toughest part can be properly communicating how much work it takes to raise a wonderful pup. The perfectly behaved pup doesn't just magically appear out of thin air! You might have to remind non-dog-lovers that dogs are only as good as their owners. Pups need you to be consistent and calm so that they, in turn, are inspired to be on their best behavior. And as you're navigating how to be the best dog mom you can be, it's possible that you'll have to be more absent socially than you'd like to be.

It can also be difficult to make it clear that while it might be not strictly life-threateningly necessary to go home and let your pup out right after happy hour, you didn't get a dog so that he or she could be cooped up all alone in a crate all evening. And, of course, you love this fur babe. You want to soak every ounce of time that you have with him or her, which can be limited in a world of work and commutes and networking events.

CONVERTING THE MASSES

If you can get your friends on board, it's possible to have the best of all worlds. Here are a few tried-and-true strategies to get those non-dog moms warmed up to your pup in no time. You might even be able to turn them into a trusted dog aunt!

- Invite your friends along to activities that are just more fun with a pup, like going on a hike or having a picnic at a nearby park.

- If you and your friends are searching for activities to share that don't involve spending money or drinking alcohol, go on a walk through the park or around a new neighborhood with your pup together. Taking a walk together is a great way to be active and still be able to catch up on all of the latest gossip, and it's the perfect way to incorporate your pooch into the plans.

- Take them to the Shangri-La of dog owners everywhere: those spots that are overcome with adorable pooches of all ages and breeds. This could be the local park before 9am on a Saturday morning (when off-leash time is allowed), or the nearby dog beach that is covered with four-legged friends frolicking in the surf. It's hard not to fall in love with all of those pups happily coexisting in the closest thing to dog heaven!

- Be respectful of your friend's personal space. Some people just aren't comfortable having a dog next to them on the couch, and some people who have had past negative experiences with mean dogs can be triggered by a dog jumping on them (even if your pup is only trying to cover your friend in slobbery kisses). Keep your pup on a leash or very much under your control until your friend becomes comfortable.

· And if your friend is really not okay with dog contact, don't be offended! One of my husband's good friends was bitten by a dog when he was little, and he's completely terrified of Gertie, even though we know she doesn't have a violent bone in her body. The two of them in the same room is just not going to happen! If you have a friend who's scared of dogs, put your pup in another room when he or she visits your place or leave your pup at home for your plans together. It can also be helpful to take it super slowly. One of my friends was scared of pups, and we first worked at her just being in the same room with Gertie on a leash, and then just gently patting her on the back while I held her, before we finally got to my friend actually petting her and being okay with being in the same room with her. Phobias and traumatic experiences are very real, so be respectful and compassionate, even if you know your pooch would never hurt a soul.

PART IV

STAYING HEALTHY AND LOOKING FAB

Fun, Fashion,
and Food

ONLY THE BEST FOR YOUR BABE

· · · · · · · · · · ·

One of the big parts of being a dog mom: wanting to give your pup all the finer things in life. You want to give your dog the best life possible, full of entertaining objects and thrilling experiences. You didn't get a dog to guard your house; you got a pup to snuggle up with you while watching romantic comedies and to come with you to sip bottomless mimosas at brunch. Duh!

Sure, all a pup needs are food, water, love, and some room to run, but part of the fun of being a dog mom is splashing out on things that your dog will love and that you'll get a kick out of.

CREATING YOUR PUP'S PERFECT HOME

Dogs spend more than half of their time sleeping; for some breeds, it can be up to 80 percent of their days! Although they can certainly flop down anywhere for a nap, they definitely prefer to have an outrageously comfortable spot to snooze. And they are naturally den animals, which means they love having a cozy little space of their own. For the dog mom, those little nooks can be fun new spots to decorate!

PINTEREST-WORTHY CRATES

Crates are super helpful training tools, especially for new puppies, but all dogs want a cozy napping spot. And if you don't want your dog child taking over the most comfortable corners of your home, you'll have to craft them their own dedicated spots; after all, they deserve five-star style and comfort.

The modern dog's ancestors had to seek refuge from predators, so it's in their DNA to be most comfortable in enclosed spaces. The crate is their modern den, where they can let their tail down and relax.

Gert's crate is her "room," and we treat it as such. Although we tuck it underneath the stairs à la Harry Potter, it is much more luxurious than Harry's cupboard. It's draped with her colorful Mexican serape blanket so that it stays dark and cool inside, lined with a furry blanket for prime napping, and looks like a fun little corner of our home from the outside. It's also her safe space. If she heads in of her own accord to take a nap, we try our hardest not to bother her. All of the work to make it comfortable pays off: she often chooses her crate over her fancy dog bed for an afternoon nap, and it usually takes some enticing to get her to leave it in the morning.

Comfort is key. Keep the bottom lined with a plush towel or even a soft dog bed. No dog wants to sleep on the cold metal wire or the basic plastic tray that comes standard in most crates. Having something that's easy to take out and throw in the washing machine makes it easier to keep it smelling fresh and clean in there, too!

Decor. The possibilities are endless! Finding a subtle, neutral-colored sheet to drape over the crate can help it blend in with the rest of your design. You can also opt for a more vividly colored, patterned, or striped blanket or sheet to make it stand out in the room.

Toys. Whenever you put your dog in the crate, make sure he or she has at least two toys: one for chewing and one for snuggling. Giving your pup a couple of treats whenever you put him in the crate can also help create a strong positive association with the space, especially if you're leaving him for the day or night. After Gert's last late-night walk, all we have to do is get out a treat and she immediately waltzes over to her crate and snuggles up. It's her cue that it's time for her bedtime treat!

Handmade dog blanket. My grandmother once crocheted an afghan specifically for my childhood dog, Susie. It was in shades of brown to match her brindled coat. However, even if it's not color-coordinated to match your dog's coat, a blanket just for him or her is essential, whether it's kept in the pup's bed or crate, or it's draped over your couch cushions to protect them from pup nails that might snag.

Specially made dog teepee. Having a teepee for your pup is perhaps superfluous, but they're so much fun! Etsy has a ton of options for artisan-crafted dog teepees. They're similar to crates, in that pups can happily curl up in them and feel extra safe and cozy. If your space is extra sunny during the day, a teepee can also be a nice, naturally darker space for your dog's afternoon naps.

MY DOG IS NOT SPOILED, I'M JUST WELL TRAINED

GIVING YOUR PUP
ALL OF THE FUN

Toys, toys, toys! Toys are an integral part of a dog's life, keeping her active and engaged! And as we like to say, a tired dog means happy owners (and unchewed corners of couches). A lot of toys are designed to mimic the ancient hunting and foraging behaviors of dogs' wild canine ancestors: catching, fetching, and shaking the "prey" can be very satisfying for a pup.

Like any good parent, you want your pup to have a well-rounded selection of playthings: toys that will make them smarter, faster, stronger, happier. And any good dog mom knows it's important to spoil your pup! Your baby has to have the best of the best and the newest toy on the block. New waterproof Frisbee? You bet! Automatic ball thrower? A must have.

Chew toys. To keep his teeth strong and healthy (and your shoes and couch cushions intact), make sure your pup has plenty of proper things to chew. Think dental bones, cow hooves, antlers, and pig ears of all textures and sizes. Gert's especially partial to Benebone wishbones. Made of super-strong nylon and food-grade bacon, one bone can keep her happily busy for hours. However, note that some chew toys can be tougher on stomachs than others.

Cuddle toys. Just like dog moms, fur babes have natural nurturing instincts. Make sure they have soft stuffed toys to snuggle up with. There are infinite options now: stuffed dogs that look just like them, desserts, pizza slices, even emojis!

Toys to fetch. Similar to those nurturing instincts, most pups have a natural desire to fetch, though this is more programmed in some dogs than others (helloooo, Labrador retriever moms!). A standard tennis ball will usually do the trick, although you might want to buy in bulk if your pup is particularly slobbery or if you're playing outside; tennis balls are fairly cheap, and they can get gross and muddy fast. But if you want to step it up a notch, just find a ball that also squeaks; no dog can resist! A Frisbee can be another excellent way to satisfy those fetching instincts, especially for a doggo that loves to go long and jump. And if your pup is a particularly avid fetcher or an especially energetic athlete, a ChuckIt! ball thrower to make that ball go extraaaaaa long is a must-have.

Educational toys. What dog mom doesn't believe that her own pup is just as smart as any next honor roll student? Invest in some toys where you can hide a treat inside; this will keep your dog's body and mind busy. We actually make Gert work for her dinner: She gets fed either from a maze bowl that stimulates her brain and reduces the danger of bloat by slowing down her eating, or from a toy that she has to keep moving on its rocker to get her kibble to fall out one piece at a time. I like to think we're creating a genius dog, as well as maintaining the ultimate slim pug.

KEEPING IT ALL ORGANIZED

The easy work is splurging on all of those super-fun toys. Figuring out a stylish solution to store all of those rope bones and squeaky donuts and tennis balls? That's another story. It's easy for all of those whimsical must-haves to take over your living room. We have a beautiful handwoven Ugandan basket for all of Gert's toys. That makes it more palatable for her to have so many toys and helps us keep the number of toys in check. Plus, her favorite game is to stand on her hind legs to knock the top off the basket!

Other cute ideas for toy storage solutions include a pretty wicker laundry basket that doesn't have a top (easier for your pup to grab his favorites, and easier for you to toss them back in), a colorful kids' hamper, a classic children's toy chest, or a wooden wine crate (you can stain it to blend in with the rest of your furniture).

The key rule of decluttering (thank you, KonMari) is to get rid of anything that doesn't spark joy. So, if there's a toy that your dog has been neglecting lately—or never really took to—get rid of it! Just like kids, dogs grow out of certain toys, and with a constant stream of new ones, there's no use keeping them all forever.

That said, however, I will confess that Gert has a stuffed turtle that I don't think we'll ever be able to part with. It was her very first toy, and we still remember when it was twice as big as she was! She still loves it, and even though it's starting to lose its original fluff and flair, it's certainly our sentimental favorite.

DRESS TO IMPRESS

Your dog's collar, harness, and leash are the building blocks of the rest of her style. Think of it as a uniform: It's what a dog wears every day and the first thing that announces her presence and personality to the rest of the world. And as a dog mom, it's also an extension of your style and your values. You know that pup's gotta look as good as her mama! Some paw-pular uniform ideas include:

The fashionista. Your mantra is quality over quantity when it comes to fashion. Your rescued Rhodesian ridgeback mix wears a gorgeous cognac leather collar with matching leash.

The prep. Think handwritten thank-you notes, week-ends at the shore, and perfectly pressed collars. Your golden retriever sports a blue-and-white seersucker collar in the summer months, and a classic navy with a bow-tie in winter.

The world traveler. Matching everything, from your hot pink phone case, hot pink carry on, hot pink passport holder, and various other Caribbean-colored accessories. Your adorable pug gets the same treatment with matching collar, leash, and carry-on carrier bag! With comfortable shoes and frequent flier miles, the two of you are ready for any adventure.

The punk. A studded collar on your all-black pup matches your black nails and fierce personality.

The sports fan. Your chocolate lab is ready for all seasons—sports season, that is—with a football jersey, basketball jersey, baseball tee, and hockey jersey that proudly proclaim your team allegiance.

ADDING ON WITH ACCESSORIES

Having a stylish collar, harness, and leash is just the beginning, of course. There are endless ways to up your pup's style game.

THE BASICS

These are the practical considerations any dog mom must take into account to keep her pup comfortable and cozy. Every dog mom has at least these essentials in her closet:

Sweaters and pup parkas. In cold climates, dog sweaters and pup parkas are a necessity when temperatures start to drop. You'll likely want sweaters in a variety of colors and patterns, and outerwear to match the climate: perhaps a slick yellow rain jacket or a puffy pink parka (or both!).

Snow boots and snow socks. And in big cities with snow, adorable snow boots or snow socks are essential to protect paws from salted sidewalks. You might want to have your camera phone ready to record the first time you put socks or shoes on your pup, though. The herky-jerky reactions as they try to figure what exactly is on their paw can be hilarious.

Cooling bandanas. For the hot dog days of summer, there are cooling bandanas in plenty of shades, a festive way to hide an ice pack near your pup's neck and chest.

EVERYDAY ACCESSORY FUN

Any dog mom knows that dressing your dog can be pure fun, whether it's a funny T-shirt or a full-blown costume. Don't be afraid to go a little overboard!

T-shirts. A few popular sayings include:
- Mama's Good Boy
- Fur Baby
- I'm Here to Paw-ty
- Feast Mode
- Bad to the Bone
- Ruff Life
- Voted Most Paw-pular

Bright bowties. To step up your pup's look from fine to fancy instantly, add a bowtie to his or her collar. These quirky and creative details instantly make your dog stand out in a crowd, whether it's for a day of window shopping on Main Street or a formal affair. It's a classy look for both boys and girls. Gert wore a white bowtie collar with a white leash for our wedding, and she was the talk of the town!

Bandanas. Bandanas give you an easy way to update your pet's look, and there are endless variations: patriotic and sports-themed, colorful and kitschy, solid and patterned. You can even make them yourself from old fabric scraps or T-shirts! If you're less of DIY mama, check out Etsy or your local pet boutique for a plentiful selection of options.

Hair clips. Hair clips can be adorned with a wide variety of flirty options, from brightly colored bows to floral accents. Note that your pup has to have a certain type of fur to truly accommodate these!

TURNING IT UP TO ELEVEN: SPECIAL OCCASIONS

. . . .

Beyond the everyday looks, no dog mom can resist designing a special runway style for a big event. There are so many different opportunities, I suggest you try them all!

BIRTHDAYS

When it comes to dog birthdays, who can resist a reason for a paw-ty? Your fur baby deserves to be celebrated and spoiled! It goes without saying that it's a day for new toys and treats, and perhaps even a splurge on a spa treatment: a paw-dicure, or a bath and blow-dry (perhaps with a blueberry facial add-on to pamper that doggy face?). And to make sure your pet is recognized as the king or queen of the day, a birthday crown never hurt!

Step it up a notch with canine-friendly baked goods for your pup and his four-legged friends. Peanut butter pupcakes, pumpkin cinnamon cake, and ginger cookies shaped like pawprints all make for festive party food. You can bake them yourself, but make sure you stay away from dog-toxic ingredients like sugar, chocolate, butter, caffeine, grapes, raisins, macadamia nuts, and avocados. If you're not much of a chef, make a beeline to your nearest dog bakery (yes, they exist!) or just stock up on a variety of treats.

For the human friends who want to celebrate the birthday boy or girl, whip up a batch of cupcakes topped with icing paw prints or frosting replications of your dog's face, or order a custom cake imprinted with a favorite photo of the birthday pup.

You can even choose the best day to celebrate: your pup's actual day of birth, the day you chose her from the litter, the day you brought him home, or the day the adoption was finalized—or all of the above!

HOLIDAYS

Every day can be a holiday when you have a dog and a healthy supply of costumes (or just plenty of creativity).

Sure, there are the big ones. The entire month of October calls for Halloween costumes of all kinds: mummies, zombies, witches, pumpkins, or the most popular meme of the year.

Thanksgiving calls for a dog disguised as a plump turkey, a pilgrim, or a cornucopia.

December is the perfect time to break out the red and white Santa Claus suit, reindeer antlers, elf uniforms, and ugly Christmas and Hanukkah sweaters.

Don't be afraid to think beyond the basics, though. Every day is a holiday for something! Your dog loves those sparkly "Happy New Year" headbands as much as you do. A striped and star-spangled red, white, and blue bandana is perfect for the fourth of July *and* Flag Day. Dogs make perfect little leprechauns when decked out in green and covered in shamrocks on St. Patrick's Day.

Also, every sports season provides myriad opportunities! Deck your pup out in team colors, mini-jerseys of your favorite players, or even as the ball itself. Who doesn't want to see a fervent four-legged fan cheering along at your local sports bar or Super Bowl party?

My personal favorite is National Taco Day! Gert makes a *muy bonita* pug taco, complete with mini sombrero.

And, of course, mark August 26 in your calendar. That's National Dog Day! Even if a costume isn't warranted, it's still a holiday worth celebrating. For the young'uns (or even if you just need an excuse to break out the puppy photos on social media), March 23 is National Puppy Day. If you need yet another reason to fete your fur babe, all of the major dog breeds have a national day of celebration, and mixed breeds even have two! If you're not quite sure of the provenance of your pup, National Mutt Day is recognized on both July 31 and December 2.

COSTUME INSPO
IDEAS TO GET STARTED

These are usually completely impractical, but absolutely necessary. Costumes can bring a dog mom (as well as her friends, Instagram followers, and strangers on the street) lots of joy. Gert's been a pug taco (complete with a little black sombrero), a little Santa Claus, a scallywag pirate, and the toughest sheriff in town.

Of course, it's easy to buy just about any dog costume you can dream of. But if you don't want your pup looking like every other dog in the pet store, see what you can pull together yourself. There's no limit to a dog mom's crafting and creativity when it comes to dressing up her pup. Here are a few ideas to get you started:

- Where's Waldo: red and white striped T-shirt
- S'mores: add some brown felt to a white dog T-shirt, and then attach a piece of cardboard to the top
- Case of La Croix (or beer!): all you need are scissors and tape
- Piñata: lots of colorful shredded paper is needed

And it's even more fun when you and your pup are a matching pair!

- Horse and cowboy
- Lion and zookeeper
- Hot dog and concession usher (or baseball player)
- Prince Charming and Snow White
- Big Bad Wolf and Little Red Riding Hood
- Toto and Dorothy (and the Scarecrow, or the Lion)
- Sebastian the Crab and the Little Mermaid

DIET

• • •

Just like humans, dogs are what they eat. A well-balanced diet helps your fur baby stay happy, healthy, and full of energy. Beyond just keeping them svelte and light on their feet, it can also help their coats stay soft and shiny, their joints lubricated, their muscles and bones strong. And, on the other hand, food lacking in proper nutrients can lead to your doggo being overweight, lethargic, and dispirited.

The problem is that so much of the dog food on the market is the canine equivalent of McDonald's: easy, convenient, heavy on chicken by-products, and low on nutritional value.

Taking the time to read the label is the first step. What's actually in that dry kibble or can of wet food? The same way you double-check the nutritional value and ingredient list on your own grocery list, it's worth taking a closer look at what your pup is eating, especially since a dog's diet will consist almost exclusively of whatever food ends up passing your label test. At the very least, it's good to recognize (and be able to pronounce) every ingredient that is in your pup's kibble.

RAW FOOD

Inspired by natural canine diets, there are several options of raw diets for dogs. Eating a minimally processed diet is the healthiest for any species, and getting your domesticated pup closer to the carnivorous habits of their wild wolf forefathers can result in a shinier, healthier coat, better digestion, improved weight control, reduction of allergies, and more energy and stamina. If you have a dog with allergies or a sensitive stomach, raw food diets can be especially helpful.

There are several companies now that will send fresh, high-quality, vital meat-based meals straight to your door, often with USDA-approved, human-grade ingredients. Many will create customized plans specifically for your pup's size, breed, and any dietary restrictions. The meals will be delivered to your home on a regular basis so that your pup doesn't ingest any preservatives.

If you want to take your pup's diet into your own hands, there are lots of DIY raw food recipes. Although cooking raw food might seem like an oxymoron, it does involve a good amount of research, preparation, and creativity. A meal consists mostly of raw meat (duh!) and bones, and is supplemented by fruits and vegetables. Some people like to add grains to their recipes for consistency and flavor, but it's not really necessary because dogs don't need to eat grain! This sort of diet doesn't have much of a shelf life, so it will need to be prepared fresh for each meal, or frozen in batches and properly defrosted before your fur baby can enjoy.

HUMAN FOOD

It's every dog mom's prerogative to decide whether or not her fur baby should be given human food. It's no secret that every pup is going to vote a strong yes on whether he or she should be allowed table scraps! To avoid begging, though, try to resist giving your pup human food right off your plate when you're sitting at the dinner table.

The most important thing to remember is the list of foods that are toxic to dogs: alcohol, avocado, chocolate, coffee, caffeine, citrus, coconut, coconut oil, grapes, raisins, macadamia nuts, milk, dairy, nuts, onions, garlic, chives, salt, salty snack foods, and yeast dough. Never give any of those foods to your pup, and be extra careful to make sure they don't accidentally drop to the floor where your doggo can snatch them up!

That said, there are foods that aren't on the "toxic list" that can still give your pup some problems. Always test out new foods in small quantities and keep an eye on their digestion to see how foods agree with your dog.

But there are plenty of other human foods that are both enjoyable and healthful for pups.

Peanut butter. Peanut butter is full of healthy fats. Just make sure to avoid varieties that are high in sugar.

Carrots. Carrots are high in fiber and fun for dogs to chew. Share a baby carrot off your crudite plate, or cut off a slice when you're peeling and prepping carrots for dinner. Bonus: They're great for your pup's teeth! Gert doesn't beg very often, but if she spots a carrot on the cutting board or in a coworker's lunch, all bets are off.

Yogurt. If your pup has been extra smelly lately, yogurt can help with doggy flatulence! Let your pup lick the top of your yogurt lid next time you enjoy some, or top his kibble with a small spoonful. Just make that your yogurt of choice doesn't have any toxic ingredients like chocolate or a ton of added sugar.

Pumpkin. This Halloween squash is another good source of fiber and can help keep a pup's digestive tract clear. Canned pumpkin is another thing that you can use to fill and freeze in a hollow toy to delight your dog, and it can be used as an ingredient in DIY pup-friendly baked goods. Your fur baby loves pumpkin spice everything just as much as you do!

Apples. Apple can clean residue off your doggo's teeth, which can also freshen breath. Apple slices can also be a crisp and delicious treat!

Blueberries. Unlike children, dogs are often encouraged to play with their food, and blueberries can be little balls for them to chase. They're also full of antioxidants: a superfood for pups as well as humans!

Chicken. Cooked chicken is a good source of protein and a sumptuous addition to your pup's regular dog food. If you ever run out of kibble, boiling and shredding some chicken (without adding any salt, pepper, or butter) can be a great substitute. It's hard for me to resist giving Gert a couple of pieces from the breast meat whenever we get a rotisserie chicken: it might be her number one favorite human food.

Oatmeal. For aging dogs, plain oatmeal is very easy to digest and can help keep their digestion regular. If you have an older pup who's having trouble chewing hard kibble or keeping other foods down, try supplementing her diet with some cooked oatmeal.

Eggs. Eggs also have plenty of protein and healthy fats. When you concoct a Sunday morning omelette for yourself, whip up an egg for your fur baby, too; just keep it light on butter or cooking oil, and don't add any salt, pepper, or other spices. Every Saturday morning, my dad plays golf. My mom stays home to catch up on the newspaper, clean the house, and have a feast of buttered toast and eggs over easy: two eggs for her, and one egg for Annie, her Staffordshire terrier–Australian cattle dog mix. My mother is a true dog mom; if there are only two eggs left in the carton, it's one for my mom and one for Annie!

TREATS

Having a wide range of treats is important! Just like you wouldn't want to have apple pie for dessert for every meal of every day (or only flourless chocolate cake, or only snickerdoodles), variety is the spice of life for your pooch.

Having a standard soft training treat on hand is essential: something that's small and low in calories (and not too high in sugar or fat). They're obviously great when you're training a pup (aka giving them all of the treats as rewards for everything that even has a hint of being good). It can also be helpful to keep treats like this in a carrier that attaches to your pup's leash so that they're always on hand. I feel much more confident letting Gert off leash in the park if I have treats on hand; if she doesn't return when I say, "Come," she'll immediately sprint to me if I say, "Treats!"

We usually keep a few different sweets on hand in Gert's "treat jar" on our kitchen counter.

Pill pockets. Soft pill pockets are a necessity to help monthly doses of heartworm and flea medicines go down without a fight. They're also great when you're training a pup, because you can tear off little pieces and reward every good deed without breaking the diet bank.

Dental bones. Greenies or other brands of dental bones are win-wins for every pooch: your dog will love the taste, and you'll rest easy knowing that it's helping to keep their teeth and gums clean and healthy. We give Gert a dental bone for her lunch every day. One time when we were staying with my in-laws, my mother-in-law was very concerned that Gertie had "lost" her dental bone; she gave it to her, and then she didn't see it again! She looked all over the apartment to see where it could have gone. We had to reassure her that the only place it was lost was in Gert's belly. She wolfs those things down!

Milk-Bones. Milk-Bones or other grain-free hard treats are a favorite to put inside of Gert's treat ball. I find that the traditional bone shape makes it a little trickier for her to get it out, meaning she is happily occupied even longer.

Training treats. Training treats are tiny enough (and low enough in calories) that you can give several without feeling guilty, so they're perfect to reward every time your fur baby behaves (or almost behaves). Gert is particularly partial to Zuke's, which are grain-free and gluten-free and full of real ingredients like chicken, peas, chickpeas, and flaxseed. And at 1.5 calories each, they don't make us feel guilty about her being such a good girl!

DIY training treats. Everything tastes better when it's baked at home with love, and dog treats are no exception. Next time you turn on the oven and pull out the KitchenAid, consider whipping up a batch of homemade treats for your fur baby. Your pet will be happy to help out by licking the bowl clean for you, and keeping a close eye on the oven as they bake. Bonus: DIY dog treats are actually pretty easy to make and can be made with ingredients that you can usually find in the back of your pantry.

SUPPLEMENTS

Just as with humans, you can add vitamins and supplements to your pup's diet to make up for any nutritional deficiencies or to boost your pets' health as they age.

If your pup is a little overactive, try a calming supplement: chamomile, passionflower, and hawthorn berry can promote relaxation and reduce nervousness (just like your mug of chamomile tea before bed does).

If you have a doggo who constantly eats grass to self-medicate an upset tummy, try a supplement that contains chicory root, peppermint, and pumpkin. It can help aid digestion in pups with a sluggish digestive tract. Chicory root is a good source of inulin, which is a prebiotic that supports healthy gut flora in dogs.

Super-active dogs might benefit from a supplement with honey, reishi mushrooms, and spirulina. Honey not only tastes delicious but also metabolizes quickly, and reishi mushrooms promote oxygen exchange in the lungs—key for those long runs or hard sprints! Spirulina enhances exercise tolerance.

When we moved into our apartment in San Diego, we were thrilled to find out that we had a pug neighbor... and then were immediately astounded by how soft Betty Lou's coat was! Her owners let us in on the secret to her sumptuous coat: fish oil supplements! Just like humans, fish oil can help keep a dog's fur soft and joints loose; this is especially helpful for certain breeds that have problems with hips and knees, or for pups that have to go up and down a lot of stairs. It can also be beneficial for aging doggos who are suffering from arthritis. After we introduced fish oil into her diet, Gert's coat quickly became noticeably softer and shinier—so much so that we actually added fish oil to our own human supplement routine!

RECIPE INSPO:

TASTY, HOMEMADE TREATS

Although you can find many recipes online, here are two of Gert's favorites! Each recipe should yield about 20 treats, but depends on how big the cookie cutter is or how large you decide to roll them. Because there are no preservatives, you'll want to store covered in the refrigerator—or keep in the freezer and then defrost for your pup to enjoy at a later date.

DIY Pumpkin Spice Treats

- 1 cup canned pumpkin
- ½ cup peanut butter
- 2 eggs

- ¼ cup canola oil
- 1 teaspoon baking soda
- 2½ cups whole wheat flour

1. Preheat oven to 350°F.

2. Combine pumpkin, peanut butter, eggs, and oil in a bowl. Add in baking soda and whole wheat flour. Stir until a stiff dough forms. Knead dough or mix just until flour is incorporated.

3. On lightly floured surface, roll out dough about ½-inch thick with a rolling pin. Use a cookie cutter to cut out dog bone shapes (or whatever shape you prefer!), or just shape into small round balls.

4. Place on a lightly greased baking sheet at least one inch apart and bake for 15 minutes.

DIY Pupper Butter Bones

- 2½ cups flour
- 1 teaspoon baking powder
- 1 egg
- 1 cup natural peanut butter
- 1 cup water
- 2 tablespoons honey

1. Preheat oven to 350°F.

2. In a large bowl, combine flour, baking powder, and the egg. Add peanut butter, water, and honey, and stir until you have a firm, sticky dough.

3. On a lightly floured surface, roll out the dough about ½-inch thick and use a cookie cutter to make fun shapes. The treats won't spread or rise much, so get creative with your shapes and make them the size that you want them to be.

4. Place on a lightly greased baking sheet at least one inch apart and bake for 20 minutes. After they cool, give them to your pup and say, "Bone appetit!"

PART V

BEING BEST FRIENDS

How to Go Everywhere Together

GETTING AROUND IN STYLE

• •

Sure, dogs have four legs and they certainly love to use them, but sometimes they deserve to be carried in style. This is more relevant for the small pups: They *want* to go everywhere with you, but sometimes a little dog's spirit is bigger than its legs or stamina. Big dogs, on the other hand, are capable of keeping up with your stride, but might be discriminated against more boldly—no matter how good they are!

The standard carrier bag. You know the deal: It's either soft (polyester sides, mesh openings) or hard (tan plastic, wire opening), and it's generally pretty ugly. It's affordable and useful, but ugh; this is not the preferred carrier of the stylish dog mom. The upside to these boring carriers: the small and medium sizes are generally approved by TSA for use on flights (always double-check the specific size requirements of your airline before your trip), and they're widely accepted on most other forms of transit, like Amtrak. I've also found that if a dog is quietly zipped up into one of these carriers, many "no dogs allowed" restaurant patios or shopping centers will turn a blind eye. Even though these aren't the most stylish, they can be good to have on hand, especially if you're planning to use public transportation with your pup.

Doggy backpack. If you love to be active and you're worried your short-legged pooch might not be able to keep up with you, invest in a paw-some K9 Sport Sack dog backpack. It's perfect for activities like hiking and biking, and enables you to keep your hands free while your tiny pup enjoys the view from up top. On the flip side, investing in a cute cargo vest for bigger dogs means they can help carry some of the load when you're out and about.

Stroller. If you've got a pup who has a tough time walking or breathing, or tires out easily in older age, investing in a dog stroller can make all the difference. Not only will it free up your arms (and save your back) from constantly picking up and carrying your fur baby, but it's a much more luxurious and relaxing way for your pup to enjoy her time out in the world. The extra storage in a premium pet stroller can be especially helpful for dog moms on the go!

Bike basket. If you're an avid cyclist, it's essential to add on some accessories to share the pastime with your pup. Attaching a wicker basket with wire cover to the front or back of your bike can easily transform your bike into a pup chariot, although you'll likely want to line the basket with a soft blanket to make the ride extra smooth. For bigger dogs, consider attaching a bike stroller to the back. Your pup can enjoy the view and the wind rushing through his fur without having to do any of the work themselves!

The pugpoose. When we first brought home Gertie, she was six pounds of puggy delight. Before she got all of her shots, we wanted to take her with us everywhere but were worried about what she'd be able to get into on the, frankly, disgusting streets of New York City. So we invested in a pugpoose! The more conventional name might be a BabyBjörn, but pup-poose or pugpoose certainly has a nicer ring to it. The front carrier lets her see the world in front of her, but her precious little paws never have to touch the dirty sidewalks. It was especially convenient before she was completely vaccinated, but even now, it's a delightful way to travel with her on the subway or on long walks that might tire out her little puggy legs. That said, now we laugh whenever we see a baby in a pugpoose!

FINDING ACTIVITIES YOU LOVE TO DO TOGETHER

Celebrating every aspect of having a dog is part of what separates a dog mom from a dog owner. Early-morning walks, mealtimes, and training aren't just chores; they're opportunities to hang out, and to build a strong and fulfilling relationship with your number one pal.

W-A-L-K-S

Of course, walking the dog is an essential part of being a dog owner. But for the dog mom, finding that favorite outing spot can make for plenty of fulfilling adventures, whether it's a walk along a nearby creek, an early-morning frolic in an empty park, or a sunset walk along the beach (just as romantic when it's with your dog, to be honest).

If you live in an area with lots of dog-friendly boutiques, taking your pup as you window shop or run errands can be a nice way to squeeze in extra steps as well.

ORGANIZE A DOG PLAYGROUP

Just like humans, dogs are social creatures: they love having a group of friends! Finding other dog moms can be such a blessing. You can trade training tips and tricks while you enjoy a glass of wine and your pups tire each other out.

Setting up an ongoing playgroup can be an excellent way to build camaraderie among pups and your dog-loving girlfriends, neighbors, or coworkers. All you need is a regular time and a big, preferably enclosed space; a yard, a rooftop, or a sectioned-off area of a park will do.

THE DOG PARK

The greatest place to scout out other dog moms: your own street and your local dog park! Finding nearby dog moms is many layers of amazing. Not only do you get all of the normal dog mom benefits, but you also have someone nearby who can easily swoop in to help with walking, play-dates, or sleepovers when you need it. Don't be scared to say hello or start up a conversation.

When we first brought Gertie home, we spent a lot of time on the sidewalk outside our Brooklyn apartment trying to convince her to pee outside and not inside on our nice new hardwood floors. Having an adorable teeny-tiny pug is an easy way to make friends with strangers and we chatted with several of our neighbors on our stoop. Lo and behold, one came by a month later with an equally adorable and considerably fluffier Sheltie puppy. Gert and Quinn became the best of friends, and having another dog mom in the building was a godsend. We exchanged keys and would trade off on after-work walks when one of us was running late or had plans in the city, or we'd both grab a glass of wine and head up to the common rooftop to tire out our pups before dinner.

When we moved to San Diego and spotted a pug pillow on a dog bed on a neighbor's patio and then noticed a real-life pug inside, we were ecstatic. There was another pug friend in the building! We quickly befriended Betty Lou's owners and now we can take evening walks together in the neighborhood, and they can advise us on all the best dog beaches in our new city.

PRO MOM TIP

Nix the ear buds! I try not to wear headphones when I'm walking Gert so that I can concentrate on her. Part of it is training-focused, but I feel no shame in admitting that I have conversations with my dog as we stroll around the neighborhood.

DOG MEET-UPS

In many big cities, there are breed-specific meet-up groups. If you're a nut for your particular type of dog, one of these can be a little circle of heaven. I go crazy for all of the snorts, smushed faces, and curly tails at pug meet-ups. Gert is stoked to play with all of those dogs who look (and often act) just like her, and I'm thrilled to be surrounded by pug people. Bonus: it's the perfect place to suss out new dog mom friends!

At 9 a.m. on the first Saturday of every month in the north end of Brooklyn's Prospect Park, you'll spot plenty of pugs as part of an ongoing Brooklyn pug meet-up. There are similar ones on different days of the month and in different spots of the park for all kinds of breeds! If you're interested in bonding with like-minded pup parents and twinning pups, check Meetup.com for breed-specific playgroups.

MAKE EVERY DAY TAKE-YOUR-DOG-TO-WORK DAY

You know what makes any and every work day better?
A four-legged friend at your desk! Having a dog-friendly
office is a win-win. Seeing a friendly pup around the
office is an enormous morale booster for just about any
coworker with a heart. And for the dog mom, getting to
have your fur baby with you all day is not only reassuring
but convenient. There's no need to schedule a dog walker
or worry about what your pup is getting up to all day!

If you don't work in a dog-friendly office, don't fret.
You might just not work in a dog-friendly office *yet*!
If you work for a small business, try bringing it up to
HR or organizing an after-work happy hour with your
coworkers—perhaps at an al fresco location where you
can bring your pup to show off his good behavior. If you
need to convince someone, there's a ton of research out
there supporting how office dogs can boost morale *and*
productivity.

I can certainly attest to all of the above. Gertie started
going to the office with me when she was 16 weeks old,
and she quickly became the star of the workplace. It
made her more comfortable in strange new environments,
friendlier with strangers, and way more independent.
And although I didn't work at crazy-big companies, Gert's
exuberance (and general puppy cuteness) forced me to
put names to various faces I'd seen around the office but
hadn't yet met. Having to take a pup out for midday walks
not only forced more steps on my pedometer app, but the
screen break also gave me more energy and inspiration.

And walking meetings with Gert were more in-demand than any conference room space!

SHARING THE LOVE

. . . .

If your camera roll is completely full of pictures of your pup and your own social media is less about your life and more about tracking all of the adorable things your fur babe does in a day (Wake up! Take a nap! Roll in a pile of leaves! Go back to sleep!), it might be time to craft a social media profile dedicated to your dog. Sure, you might feel a little ridiculous—but all of those aww-worthy snaps deserve to be seen and admired, by friends and strangers alike.

The first step: choosing a handle. You'll want something that's catchy and memorable; it might include your pup's name, sum up his personality, or pay tribute to his breed—or ideally does all three!

The next step: figuring out how to distill your pup's personality into his or her social media voice. Is your dog a true derp, prone to a lot of wide eyes, tilted head, and questioning expressions? Or is your fur child a sophisticated savant, worthy of the Honor Roll, stuck in a floppy dog's body? What do they call you (their personal photographer and copywriter extraordinaire): Mom? Mama? Treat Lady? Figure out what sounds most authentic to your pup, and stay true to her (imagined) vernacular.

And, of course, your pup's social media feed is a prime location for any and all dog puns. Into how many captions can you squeeze in bone-a-fide dog jokes?

A few tricks for Insta-worthy photo shoots:

- Holding a squeaky toy or tennis ball just above the camera can help get your pup's attention for the paw-fect shot.

- Floppy ears and chunky rolls look especially hilarious when filmed in slo-mo.

- Take cues from traditional newborn shoots for a funny juxtaposition; for example, take photos of your puppy in the same position at the beginning of every month to document how he or she grows. Or pose for a "new family" photo with you staring lovingly into the eyes of your swaddled pup.

- For the most flattering canine portraits, get down on your dog's level. Being able to look directly into his eyes (instead of seeing the top of his head) makes for a far more compelling photo.

- Have plenty of training treats on hand! A necessary command for the digital age: training your dog on "look at me" makes getting the perfect shot easy, time after time.

INSTA INSPO:
PUPS ON THE GRAM

JIFF POM (@jiffpom): The most popular pup on Instgram, this Pomeranian has been in music videos (hello, Katy Perry!) and has more than 8 million followers. He's also the 2015 *Guinness Book of World Records* winner of "Fastest Dog on Two Paws."

DOUG THE PUG (@itsdougthepug): With more than 3 million followers, this Nashville-based pug is also very famous.

CORGNELIUS AND STUMPHREY (@corgnelius): Two stumpy-legged corgi brothers living in Los Angeles.

MARU (@marutaro): A very chill shiba inu from Japan. He has a fantastic smile.

MARNIE (@marniethedog): A shih tzu with a great story. Her owner rescued her at age 11 and helped care for her many health issues. Now she's a happy, healthy senior dog with a tongue too big for her tiny mouth.

TUNA (@tunameltsmyheart): Tuna is a Chihuahua dachshund mix (aka, a Chiweenie) whose reaction shots are priceless!

MANNY (@manny_the_frenchie): Manny claims to be the most followed bulldog on the web, for good reason. This Frenchie loves a stylish outfit and a good nap.

HARLOW, SAGE, INDIANA, AND REESE (@harlowandsage): A group of dog BFFs, featuring a very large Weimaraner and her very small miniature dachshund friends.

GERTIE (@cestgertie): Obviously, I have to include my favorite social dog, my own Gertrude Rose!

SNAIL MAIL

Although I delight in sharing real-time photos and videos of my pug, there's a certain pleasure that comes only from sending something tangible via snail mail. This is true of life in general, but particularly when it's a piece of mail that proudly features my pup's beautiful face.

Try making a custom postcard pack that features your fur baby's most model-worthy poses, like from Artifact Uprising. Then you can jot down a quick note on a super high-quality card that's graced with an image of those puppy dog eyes.

The classiest dog mom move: monogrammed stationery with a custom illustration of your pup. As a wedding gift, a wonderful friend gave me a set of linen textured notecards with my new married initials and a watercolor of a perfect fawn pug. It's my go-to stationery from now on!

And you don't have to restrict your love of your dog to the inside of the envelope. Zazzle.com makes custom stamps, so you can stick on a beautiful rendition of your pup's face instead of a boring old American flag.

And to be completely frank, my purchase of a custom hand-drawn rubber stamp portrait of Gert's face has been one of the best investments of my life. We stamped her little puggy face on the back of the envelopes of our wedding invitations and wedding thank-you notes, and now I like to plunk down the stamp on just about any piece of fun mail that I send. It's my signature pug mom move! Check out Stamp Yo Face and make a rubber stamp of your own fur baby; I promise you'll be sending more mail in no time.

BONE VOYAGE

· · · · · · · · · ·

A dog mom never wants to leave her fur baby behind, even if she's heading out on an ultra-relaxing and luxurious vacation. Although traveling with your pooch can sometimes add a layer of complication to a process that itself isn't always smooth, it can also be incredibly fun to experience a beautiful new place with your best sidekick.

Of course, the ease of traveling with your fur baby is super dependent on just how big your dog is. Tinier pups are so much more portable. Pop your pet in a carrier and take her with you (almost) anywhere! A bigger dog might require more creative solutions to transport, but that doesn't mean they make the end result any less enjoyable!

If you're considering traveling with your pup, there are a few extra things to consider beyond just beach versus mountains, craft beer versus margarita, relaxation versus adventure.

You must take your pup's travel preferences into consideration! A rural dog who's well-suited to wide open spaces might have trouble with the noise and chaos of a big city, but is likely very interested in a relaxing lake house holiday. On the other hand, a cosmopolitan pup who's used to chilly winters (and has the heavy coat to prove it) might not be as excited for 90-degree beach escapes as you are. If you're dedicated to taking your fur baby with you on your next vacation, make sure that you're going somewhere he or she will actually enjoy. If not, your pooch might prefer to stay at home on the couch with a dog sitter who will spoil them.

One unexpected bonus of crate training: It makes it really easy to travel with your dog! Gert loves her crate, and we often take it with us when we travel (especially if our destination is within driving distance). Her crate easily breaks down to be transported flat and then be put back together wherever we're sleeping for the night. She's instantly comfortable when she's sleeping in her crate, whereas she tends to be a little barkier if we let her sleep in our bed in a new environment.

DOGS
ARE MY
FAVORITE
PEOPLE

PRO MOM TIP

If your dog is certified as an emotional support animal, he or she is legally allowed to accompany you onto a flight free of charge. You do still need to alert the airline that you'll be traveling with an animal, however. It's important so that the airline may alert any people who are allergic, and many flights are capped at a certain number of animals on board. You can note that you'll be traveling with a service animal during the part of booking flights that asks if you have any special requests or if you need to alert the airline of a disability, and you'll need to carry a signed letter from your doctor designating your dog as an emotional support animal. If your pet is purely a travel companion, you'll need to invest in a TSA-approved carrier that can easily slide under the seat and your pup will need to stay completely zipped up in it the entire time they're in the airport or on the plane. Regardless of whether you have a support animal or just a loving pet, double-check all requirements with your airline before you head to the airport. You don't want to encounter any surprises!

PLANES

Pups love the window seat as much as anyone else! Taking your fur baby on his first flight can be stressful, but I promise that adorable puppies on planes (and even the occasional bark) bring so much more joy to your fellow passengers than a crying baby.

Many airlines and airports are leaning into becoming more dog-friendly. It can be worth sussing out an airport's website before you fly in or out of it, especially if your travel includes a layover. Research whether the airport has

in the room; a welcor
bones; and unlimiter
hotel staff can ever
tips on the best dc
neighborhood.

The
they v
anim
hote
limi
do
ni

t

an outdoor space for pups to frolic in or a "pet relief area"
after you go through security. If the airport doesn't have
those amenities and you have a long flight ahead of you, it
might be worth training your pup on pee pads and packing
a few extras. Either way, to avoid accidents, you might
want to pick up the water bowl early and give your pup a
smaller breakfast than usual before taking him or her on a
long-haul flight.

Gert has been racking up frequent flier miles since she
was a pup, and she's now a model traveler. She doesn't
make a peep once she's on the plane, although she's
always very happy to welcome any admiring belly rubs
from fellow passengers or flight attendants.

TRAINS

Train travel is similar to travel on airplanes: there are
usually weight and size restrictions, there will usually be
an extra fee for nonservice animals, and you'll need to
keep your fur baby zipped up in an approved carrier during
the journey.

However, train travel usually includes lots of regular
station stops that give you an opportunity to exercise
those four legs. Double-check with a conductor the length
of each stop, but it's usually possible for you at least to
pop out with your pooch for a potty break.

AUTOMOBILES

There's a reason one of the iconic "happy dog" photos
is of a pup with his head hanging out the window of the

car: Pups love t
quality time w
and smells pa
they're crossi
the pet store

Safety fi
invest in a
or purcha
harness t
or hoppi
keep yc
matter
you're

Ro
they
son
a l
ba
r

KEEP CALM

AND

LOVE DOGS

the
will now greet

RAISING A RESPONSIBLE DOG MEMBER OF SOCIETY

One of the best bits of advice that our crazy pug lady breeder gave us was, "There are no bad dogs, only bad owners."

Essentially, you have to take the initiative to educate yourself about basic dog-training principles, and you have to commit to being super consistent about enforcing rules and discipline. Dogs are mostly motivated by affection and food. In short, they can be easily trained with positive affirmations and a regular stream of treats. Of course, some breeds are more easily trainable than others. Labrador retrievers, for example, are particularly well-suited to fetching and developing a close rapport with their owners, while pugs and French bulldogs are easily persuaded to do just about anything as long as there is food involved.

There is no shortage of books, online resources, and in-person classes that will promise a pawfectly trained pup. But every dog mom knows that her pup is only as good as the training foundation and ongoing education that she can provide.

The most important thing to remember is consistency! Figure out what rules you want your pup to abide by, and stick to them—and be conscious of the behavior that you're rewarding. Think through things from the dog's point of view! If you always slip your pup a piece of meat from your meal, she'll eventually come to expect that. And if she'll only hush up with a treat, you're teaching her that barking will be rewarded.

EMOTIONAL SUPPORT ANIMAL

Emotional support animals can provide a tangible benefit to a person with a disability. They can be used for a range of needs, but in particular, their calming presence and unconditional love can be very helpful for people who suffer from depression and anxiety.

A dog doesn't need to have any formal training to be recognized as an emotional support animal, but you do need to have a certified letter from a mental health professional if you want to be able to take your pup with you as an emotional support animal on a plane or in a no-pets-allowed rental.

CERTIFIED THERAPY DOG

If you have a well-mannered dog who absolutely loves people, you shouldn't keep all of that happiness just for yourself and your friends. Getting your fur baby certified to be a therapy dog means you can spread that joy to people who need it most—in hospitals, hospices, and nursing homes.

It's not an easy or quick process to certify a therapy dog. You'll need to fill out extensive paperwork and pay membership fees, get your pup observed in a variety of settings, and commit to a regular volunteer site. Most therapy dog organizations require pups to be at least one year old before becoming certified.

Of course, not every dog is cut out to be a therapy dog, and that's totally fine. But if you're looking for an opportunity to get more involved in your community and want your super-chill pup to be a part of it, volunteering with your dog babe can be a truly rewarding experience for both of you!

We recently worked to have Gert certified as a therapy dog, and it's been an incredibly positive experience. We volunteer once a month in a senior center, and it's deeply fulfilling. I love seeing how much joy she brings to a population that doesn't often get to interact with pups!

PART VI

BUILDING YOUR COMMUNITY

It Takes a Village
to Raise a Pup

FIND YOUR TRIBE

· · · · · · · · · · · · ·

If it takes a village to raise a child, it takes a devoted community of dog aunts and uncles to raise a pup. Surrounding yourself with friends—or sometimes even acquaintances—who are passionate about your dog can ease the burden on you. These are the friends whom you can tap to dog sit when you're out of town for the weekend, or who can swing by to let your pooch out and give her some snuggles when you're held up late at work. First things first: give them a copy of your key, because I promise it will come in handy.

Finding your tribe of people who love your pup just as much as you do (well, almost as much) is good for you *and* good for your dog babe. It can help take all sorts of pressure off you: mental, physical, and financial. And just like humans, laid-back dogs who are flexible and adaptable to many different people, situations, and environments are generally less anxious and more content. Ensuring that they're not just reliant on you for all of their happiness will make things a lot easier for you and them in the long run!

And for a dog mom, it's key to have a friend whom you can text your frustrations to when your pup just won't behave—a friend who won't judge you, and who might just show up on your doorstep with a bone and a bottle of wine! It's also great to have a neighbor who can swoop in and let the dog out when you're stuck in a scream-inducing traffic jam, or a couple who can't quite swing a dog of their own but who are always up for taking care of yours for the weekend, or a coworker who's happy to tie the leash to their desk (or pop your pup on their lap) if you're in a meeting that goes long.

The reality is that, like everything else in the world, it can be hard to accept help without feeling like you're imposing, but drop that guilt! Dogs are actually givers of joy, fantastic furry creatures that reduce anxiety and stress and promote happiness and relaxation. And you, devoted mother of one of these magical beings, are generous enough to gift other people with their presence. Think back to those days before you were a dog mom: You probably would have been absolutely stoked to hang out with a four-legged friend for a while, no strings attached. Heck, you probably would have paid to do so!

If you want to sweeten the deal beyond just the gift of your pup's presence, most dog aunts won't turn down a bottle of wine or a pedicure date as thanks. Being sincerely appreciative and offering a token of your thanks will encourage your friends and neighbors to stay on the "helping out with the dog" short list. And if you're relying on another dog mom: always be ready to return the favor!

BEING A DOG AUNT

· · · · · · · · · · · · · ·

Before you become a dog mom, you often become a dog aunt. And to be honest, being a dog aunt can be all of the fun with none of the expenses or responsibilities!

Of course, the easiest way to become a dog aunt is if one of your closest friends purchases a dog, but that's not the only way! If you regularly spot a neighborhood dog, or develop a close bond with a coworker's pup, or even just sign up to take care of a stranger's fur baby on Rover, those are all opportunities to become a trusted dog aunt.

Part of being a dog aunt is frequently and enthusiastically professing not only your love for pups, but your genuine willingness and desire to take care of them. Being a reliable dog sitter (or pinch walker) who is happy to be paid just in dog licks and snuggles is an easy way to have a fur baby in your life.

FINDING YOUR DOG'S BEST DOG FRIEND

Just like with people, there are some dogs that just immediately click and others that hate each other on sight. When your dog child finds his or her new furry best friend, though, it's a wonderful feeling! It can pay off in dividends for you: A post-playdate pup is often exhausted, and thus in prime snuggle condition. And the more friends your dog has, the happier and more well-adjusted your pup will be.

DOGS LEAVE

PAW

PRINTS

ON YOUR

HEART

PRO MOM TIP

Playing canine matchmaker isn't always easy. If you're introducing your pup to a new dog, consider the temperament of each. Some dogs have better social skills than others!

Consider planning the first doggie date on neutral ground instead of at your abode or theirs, where a dog may get territorial. Let the dogs check each other out on the leash, but watch for hostile signs. Don't get involved unless things get aggressive; it's best if the dogs can do their own thing without human interaction. Once everyone begins to look friendly, unleash them (if you're in a gated space) and let the best friend bonding commence!

Part of being a great dog mom is making sure your pup is well-socialized and friendly, but to take it to the next level, you have to nurture those friendships. That means taking your fur baby to the dog park when you know his friends are going to be there, and proactively setting up additional puppy playdates with his best buds.

And if your pup hits it off with a dog who has a great dog mom, lean into the friendship! Puppy playdates can be so much more fun when you're trading dog-rearing stories over a bottle of wine or on a morning walk to grab a latte. It can also be really comforting to find a friend whom you can trust with your fur baby, and someone who totally understands all of your puppy-misbehaving frustration (and has zero judgment).

We've been super lucky at our last two apartments. I've quickly met neighbor dog moms with friendly pups who are always up for an after-work walk around the block or playdate (complete with a glass of wine).

HELICOPTER PARENT EMAILS

Even if you laugh at those tales of overbearing helicopter parents and insist you'll never be one: wait until the first time you leave your pup at home without you, amiright?!

I fall in the camp of preferring too much information to zero information, especially when it comes to taking care of pups. If you're leaving your fur baby in the care of friends or strangers, it can be really helpful to have a template email that you can easily send out with reminders about your pet's care. At the very least, confirm in writing:

· When your dog eats and how much she should have at each meal. (No one wants a pup to go hungry in their care, but you also don't want her to pack on the vacation pounds!)

· Your pup's standard going-out needs. (Will the pet sitter need to wake up at the crack of dawn, or can your pup handle a Saturday morning sleep-in?)

· If there is any medication your dog needs, and precise details on how to administer it.

· If your pet is allowed human food. (Everyone knows that bacon is the quickest way to an unfamiliar dog's heart!)

· Any weird quirks in their behavior. (Do they hate red cars? Love to eat rocks? Make a beeline for squirrels at the park?)

- When you're leaving and when you'll be back. (You don't want to be tied up discussing itinerary details on text when you're on vacation!)

And just like you would do for a kid, it can be helpful to pack an overnight bag if your pup is heading over to someone's house for a sleepover, or pull all of the doggy essentials out in the open if you have a pup sitter crashing at your place. In addition to the standard food and treats (lots of treats!), I also make sure that we always send Gertie off with certain essentials:

- An extra long lead. (This is especially helpful if you think the dog sitter may want to take your pup to the park, but you don't feel 100 percent confident about letting her off the leash. No one wants to lose the dog they're taking care of!)

- A bottle of bitter apple spray. (Make sure your little fur babe doesn't ruin anyone else's shoes or furniture.)

- A bottle of Nature's Miracle solution just in case of any accidents!

- A bully bone. (We don't give them to Gert very often, so it's a very special treat, but she's completely obsessed with them, so it can be a helpful break for a dog sitter who's not used to her energy.)

- And, of course, a few of her favorite toys and her collapsible crate.

EMAIL INSPO:

DETAILS FOR YOUR DOG SITTER

Here is the actual transcript of an email that I've sent when we went out of town and left Gertie with perfectly capable friends who love dogs. Sorry I'm not sorry I'm a crazy dog mom!

Subject Line: Taking Care of Lady Gertude

Hello!

First of all, thank you SO much for helping us out with Gertie. She's super fun and she's pretty chill—a lot less work than when she was a puppy!

A few quick questions just so that I can prep logistics properly:
- *Do you want to bring Gert over to your place, or do you want to crash at ours? No stress either way, especially since you're so close!*
- *Do you want to take her into work on Friday or leave her at home? Totally cool to leave her at home—I just want to know whether or not I should book our dogwalker (who I think you've met, ha!).*

I realize that I sound like an insane helicopter parent below, so just know that as long as she is fed and taken out and played with, she will be totally fine! Just want to give you as much info as possible.

Her general weekday schedule is below, but since you're mostly home on the weekend, know that it can be a lot more flexible based on whatever you're up to.

Holler if you have any questions before or during. I'll be in Copenhagen Wednesday through Sunday so a little less quick to respond, but David will be in Boston Thursday night through Saturday and will have full cell coverage. He's there for a wedding on Friday, so might be a little slow during the actual wedding though!

THANK YOU THANK YOU THANK YOU!

xo

GENERAL SCHEDULE

7am: *Wake up and go out*

7:30am: *Breakfast (1/2 cup of food + water)*

8:30am *or thereabouts: Go out*

1pm: *Go out + give her "lunch" (either a Greenie or a Kong stuffed with peanut butter)*

6:30pm: *Go out*

7:30pm: *Dinner (1/2 cup of food + water)*

8:30pm: *Go out*

11pm *or whenever you go to bed: Go out*

If she stands by the front door or the glass walls at Gimlet, that's usually an indication that she needs to go outside, especially if she scratches at the wall, but we're trying to train her out of doing that as a sign.

11:30pm: *In crate for bed*

COMMANDS

- *Get busy: pee or poop*
- *Sit*
- *Lie down*
- *Come*
- *Stay*
- *Roll over*
- *Shake*
- *Stand*

OUT AND ABOUT

- She's really friendly with all other dogs, but other dogs aren't always so friendly! Cool for her to always say hi, but just keep an eye out.
- Fine for her to go to dog parks, although she prefers one-on-one playdates (aka she can get a little overwhelmed with a bunch of dogs). I'm packing a super long orange leash, which is nice if you want to give her a little room to run around at a park without losing her.
- She's obsessed with rocks and leaves. Fine for her to pick them up on her walk (you likely won't be able to stop her!) but she's not allowed to bring them inside.
- I can also connect you with Shauna, our neighbor who has a sheltie named Quinn (aka Gert's best friend). They love roof dates together!
- She's great in the subway and cabs! She'll usually just sleep on your lap or in her carrier.

IF YOU NEED A BREAK

- Playing fetch with her or running her around and tiring her out is a good way to get peace later. She loves playing fetch with just about anything, and I'm sure she will exhaust herself exploring your backyard.
- Anytime you leave the apartment and when you go to sleep, she can be crated. She knows it's her little home! I usually give her a few treats and toys in her crate whenever we leave her in the crate so that she has something to occupy her.
- Before she goes to sleep, it's good to "sleep hygiene" her: Basically, you want her to be super relaxed and chill and then she'll go straight to sleep in her crate. We usually take her out (which kind of hypes her up) and then bring her back in and sit on the couch with her for 15 to 20 minutes, until she falls asleep, and then you can seamlessly put her in crate! It's also good to put a blanket over the top of the crate at night; it cues her to go straight to sleep.

The first time we left Gertie with my best friend Aly for the weekend, we sent Aly the above email and didn't worry too much about it, despite the fact that Aly didn't grow up with dogs and hadn't spent a ton of one-on-one time with Gertie. We just about died laughing when we picked Gertie up and Aly reported that at one point she had been taking a bubble bath, and that Gertie was curious about what was going on; she hopped on her hind legs to get a good look at what was going on in the bath. Aly interpreted this as Gert wanting to join her in the bath (Gertie is curious about a lot of things that she likely wouldn't actually love, ha!), so Aly picked her up and plopped her down in the bubbles. Gertie immediately freaked out and started thrashing about— quite a disturbance to Aly's relaxing evening!—and once Aly took her out of the bath, Gertie ran around like a soaked madwoman, shaking water and rolling all over the furniture.

I still laugh trying to imagine what Aly thought would happen. Did she think that Gertie would just happily settle in next to her in the bath with cucumber slices on her big buggy eyes for a bit of luxurious spa time? A spa-trained pup has to be the dream of dog moms everywhere, right?

I'M NOT A
REGULAR
MOM,
I'M A
DOG MOM

CONCLUSION

In conclusion, being a dog mom isn't for everyone. Some people are content just to own their dog: walk, feed, pick up poop, repeat. Or worse, not to own a dog. Or even worse, to own a cat! No judgment here: they can do that boring, completely unfulfilling life, and we can play the part of the crazy dog mom to perfection.

The secret to being a real dog mom isn't in the costumes you splurge on or the grain-free, gluten-free, carnivore-led raw diet you insist on feeding your pup, or in owning a super-cute graphic tee with a custom drawing of your dog's face on it. It's in the unconditional love and loyalty you give and receive from your fur babe. It's in knowing in your heart how much being a dog mom has changed you, and not trading that feeling for the world.

Real dog moms know the secret healing power of a pup. They know that wholeheartedly caring for that chosen canine can change you into a better human. You're a more patient, more loving, more lovable wife/girlfriend/partner/ daughter/best friend and perhaps even mom of humans because of it.

No matter where you adopted or purchased your pup, dogs are really the ones who rescue us. They remind us of what's important in life: to make every outing an adventure, to eat every meal with enthusiasm, to love our friends and family unconditionally and protect those loved ones fiercely. With their seven years to our every one, they remind us that life is short and that every trip to the park should be treated as if it's our last. And their pure, unbridled joy about the first walk of the day or the moment when you walk through the door after a long day of work encourages us to embrace the little everyday moments that make up a life.

So here's to the dog moms: the moms of rescues and purebreds, moms who are raising pups in teeny-tiny apartments and wide open rural spaces, first-time dog moms and several-times-over dog moms, dog moms of every age and place and style. You all are doing an out-standing job of raising those fur babies to be responsible dog citizens, and you look darn gorgeous while doing it.

Never forget that the world is a better place because of the joy that you and your pup bring into it. Dog mom life might be ruff, but it's fur-ever. And there's no other way we'd rather have it!

ACKNOWLEDGMENTS

This book was a ton of fun to write, and I'm so grateful to the people (and dogs) in my life who made it possible. First and foremost: David, for being the ultimate pug dad, husband, and coffee maker extraordinaire. Katelyn and Kate, for reading and supporting everything I do (and getting really excited about it). Jillian and Aly, for never getting sick of me talking about my dog. Erin and Megan (and all of Boat Drank), for loving dogs so deeply and being the greatest group-text cheerleaders. Mom, Dennis, and all of the Merrills, for being my biggest champions. Casie, for being a delightfully enthusiastic editor. Kourtney, for thinking of me and my crazy dog mom ways for this project. Krishna, for bringing the pups in my life to the page. And, of course, to Gertie, for making me the luckiest pug mom around.

ABOUT THE AUTHOR

Christine Amorose Merrill is a travel and lifestyle blogger who lives in San Diego with her husband and pug. Christine was born and raised in Sacramento, and earned a degree in journalism at California State University, Chico. After graduating, she lived and worked in Nice, France, and Melbourne, Australia, and backpacked solo through Europe, Southeast Asia, and Central America before spending five years working in brand partnerships in technology and media in New York City.